Walking Eye
mobile app

KU-612-796

Discover the world's best destinat... ...Guides Walking Eye app, available to download for free in the App Store and Google Play.

The container app provides easy access to fantastic free content on events and activities taking place in your current location or chosen destination, with the possibility of booking, as well as the regularly-updated Insight Guides travel blog: Inspire Me. In addition, you can purchase curated, premium destination guides through the app, which feature local highlights, hotel, bar, restaurant and shopping listings, an A to Z of practical information and more. Or purchase and download Insight Guides eBooks straight to your device.

TOP 10 ATTRACTIONS

CENTRAL HEARTLANDS
Archetypal Sweden, with a rich cultural landscape. See page 64.

SAMI
Immerse yourself in the culture of northern Europe's own indigenous people. See page 76.

SKANSEN
Step into Sweden's past at Stockholm's beautiful open-air museum. See page 34.

GOTHENBURG
Poseidon guards the great city's theatres and galleries. See page 54.

Berlitz®

SWEDEN
POCKET GUIDE

STOCKHOLM
The nation's beautiful capital, with plenty to do both on and off the water. See page 27.

VIMMERBY
Astrid Lindgren's great stories come alive here. See page 49.

MIDNIGHT SUN
Casting its light over the vast landscape of the far north, it's bright enough to play golf. See page 81.

KALMAR SLOTT
The perfect Renaissance castle, with moat, drawbridge and secret passages. See page 48.

MALMÖ
Sweden's third city, and a dazzling mixture

KIRUNA AND BEYOND
Sample some of the most remote and beautiful scenery anywhere in the world. See

A PERFECT TOUR

Day 1

Gothenburg

Kids will love Liseberg's rollercoasters and Universeum. Others should take a boat tour of the canals, then walk down Avenyn to Röhsska Museet. Enjoy gourmet seafood, then round the day off with a archipelago cruise.

Day 3

Mysteries and murders

Continue up the craggy coastline to the enigmatic Bronze-Age rock carvings at Tanum. A short way north, the picturesque fishing village Fjällbacka is the setting for several Camilla Läckberg thrillers. Those blessed with time can sail from here to Sweden's most westerly islands, the Väderöarna. Otherwise turn back for Gothenburg.

Days 4-5

Stockholm

Get a train to Stockholm. Explore medieval Gamla Stan and modern shopping streets, then visit City Hall. Devote the next day to culture: must-sees are Vasamuseet, Skansen, Fotografiska and ABBA the Museum.

Day 2

Sweden's 'summer capital'

Get a taste of the beautiful Bohuslän coast by taking the bus to Marstrand, Sweden's favourite summer resort. Explore the imposing Carlsten's Fortress, potter around the town's craft galleries, lunch on smoked prawns or fish and do a spot of afternoon sea bathing.

Day 7

Ancient Uppsala

A 40-minute train ride will take you to Sweden's birthplace. First visit the ancient burial mounds at Gamla Uppsala, a delight for Viking buffs. Head back to town for lunch, then spend the afternoon investigating the Gothic cathedral and the Gustavianum's creepy anatomical theatre.

Day 8

Heaven and hell

Catch the 8am train to Falun and spend the morning underground at Falun copper mine, the hellish source of Sweden's ancient wealth. After lunch, take bus 237 to the heavenly Carl Larsson-Gården in Sundborn, the birthplace of modern Swedish design.

Day 9

Lake Siljan, Dalarna

Hire a car or taxi in Falun, then head for the Björkberget tower near Siljansnäs for 360-degree views. Continue clockwise for the Zorn Museum and the Vasaloppet Museum, then nip up to Orsa to visit the bear park and lunch at its panoramic café. Further round the lake, stop at Nusnäs to buy brightly painted Dala horses.

Day 6

Steamship fun

Explore Stockholm's watery surroundings with a day-long steamship excursion: choose between a visit to the 17th-century Drottningholm Palace, home of the Swedish royal family; or head for the lovely town of Mariefred and stunning Gripsholm Castle.

CONTENTS

INTRODUCTION

Sweden is the largest country in Scandinavia, yet is home to just 9.8 million people. Stretching almost 1,600km from top to bottom, it entices visitors with the bustling cities of Stockholm, Göteborg (Gothenburg) and Malmö; sparkling lakes and sunny beaches; rural regions where the old songs and stories are kept alive; and the vast Arctic wilderness with its Northern Lights and annual recreation of the Ice Hotel.

GEOGRAPHY AND LANDSCAPE

At 449,964 sq km (173,732 sq miles), Sweden is the third-largest country in Western Europe – slightly bigger than California. Around half of it is surrounded by water: the Skagerrak, Kattegat and Öresund straits lie to the southwest, while the waves of the Baltic Sea roll in on the east. Much of Sweden's western side nestles next to Norway, while in the northeast the great river Torneälven marks the border with Finland. To fly over Sweden is to soar over 3,200km of wiggling coastline, countless scattered islands, miles of unspoiled countryside, deep green forests, glinting rivers and huge lakes like Vänern and Vättern, which are more like inland seas.

Winter warmer

Swedish winters are much less harsh than people might imagine, thanks to the warming influence of the Gulf Stream. December, with its traditional markets, brightly decorated streets and St Lucia processions, can be a magical time of year.

VARIED ATTRACTIONS

Even the three largest cities have plenty of green spaces. Stockholm, with a population of over 910,000, is a city of sea, lake and leafy parkland. It floats serenely on 14 islands: head eastwards and the archipelago breaks into thousands more, scattering out towards the Baltic. If you arrive by boat from Western Europe, the magnificent west-coast harbour of Göteborg (Gothenburg) is the first view. This is Sweden's second city, noted for its wide avenues and 17th-century canals. The third city, Malmö, in the far south, has a strong Danish influence, and is linked to its neighbour by a dreamlike bridge, stretching 8km across the sea.

As well as these three principal cities, there are the two university towns. Lund, near Malmö, has a venerable medieval history; while Uppsala, north of Stockholm, was once the country's ancient capital and home of the old pagan ways.

The Birka Viking museum

The farther north you travel, the emptier the land becomes. At the end of the scenic Inlandsbanan rail route are the mountains, many with a year-round covering of snow. Roughly 15 percent of the country lies beyond the Arctic Circle, where the sun refuses to set for part of each summer, and in winter the nights are similarly unending. This is also the home of Scandinavia's indigenous people, the Sami, whose wanderings with their reindeer herds take little account of national boundaries.

Sweden is strong on cultural pursuits. The country is dotted with historical surprises, including some 200 castles, palaces and country estates, as well as unique Bronze-Age rock carvings and fascinating Viking sites like the trading post Birka or the Ales Stenar ship setting. Contemporary Swedish design is everywhere:

Waving the flag on National Day

trace its roots at the home of Carl Larsson, one of the artists who inspired its clean lines and calming colours. On the musical front, Gothenburg's Symphony Orchestra is in the top rank of world orchestras, and in summer a burgeoning number of music festivals celebrate everything from chamber music to heavy metal. Sweden has even become a centre of gastronomic excellence, with 18 Michelin-starred restaurants and a countrywide pride in top-notch local produce.

RURAL ROOTS

The landscape itself has done much to shape modern Sweden. The country is well known for its consensus society, in which everybody has a say. At the root of this need for consensus is Sweden's closeness to its agrarian past. Just four or five generations ago, at the beginning of the 20th century, Sweden was an impoverished rural society, with some 80 percent of the population scratching a living from the land. Small communities had to pull together to survive the worst that nature could throw at them.

Yet in barely one hundred years, Sweden transformed itself into one of the world's richest countries, with a large number of people moving from outlying areas into the cities. Today, however sophisticated and urban Swedish city-dwellers may seem, their ties to the land remain as strong as ever. The country's much-envied cradle-to-grave social welfare system grew from a need to provide for the rural poor, and has endured from its 18th-century roots into modern times.

OUTDOOR PLEASURES

Swedes are passionate about the great outdoors and all things natural. Whether it's summer or winter, they love to go walking, skiing, climbing or, best of all, to immerse themselves in a lake or sea. An enduring image of Sweden is the *stuga*, the little red wooden house out in the countryside, where Swedish families go to kick off their shoes, swim naked and bond with nature. Among the most popular pastimes are late-summer expeditions to pick wild mushrooms and a multitude of berries, including *lingonbär* (similar to redcurrants), *blåbär* (blueberries), *hjortron* (cloudberries), *björnbär* (blackberries) and *smultron* (wild strawberries).

Another symbol of Sweden's beloved rural past is the open-air museum. The idea began in 1891, when the far-sighted Artur Hazelius realised that the Industrial Revolution was rapidly

SWEDISH CRIME FICTION

Scandinavian thriller writers have taken the world by storm with the creation of a new category of crime fiction – 'Nordic Noir'. The first Swede to exploit the country's cool, empty landscapes and small communities to creepy effect was Kerstin Ekman in her book *Blackwater*, based on a true story. Åsa Larsson, who was raised in Kiruna, also uses Sweden's far north as the backdrop to her popular Rebecka Martinsson series. A third female author, Camilla Läckberg, is a consistent Swedish chart-topper, with eight books translated into English. Henning Mankell's Inspector Wallander books are some of the most well known outside Sweden, popularised by the BBC dramatisation starring Kenneth Branagh. And Stieg Larsson's thrillers *The Girl With The Dragon Tattoo*, *The Girl Who Played With Fire* and *The Girl Who Kicked The Hornet's Nest* have sold an incredible 80 million copies since the first book was published posthumously in 2005. The fourth novel in the series *The Girl in the Spider's Web* authored by David Lagercrantz hit the shelves in 2015.

transforming Sweden. He began to 'collect' characteristic old buildings from different regions, reassembling them in natural groups at Skansen (Stockholm). Today, communities everywhere have similar collections where, in summer and on special occasions, locals don old-time costumes and dance to fiddle tunes handed down through the centuries.

PARTYING AND CELEBRATIONS

A strangely contradictory attitude to alcohol exists in Sweden. Shops and supermarkets are only permitted to sell low-alcohol beer (lättöl), and Swedes must visit the government-run Systembolaget off-licences to buy wines, stronger beers and spirits. Yet in spite of the vague feeling of prohibition that this system creates, Swedes really do love to party. Stockholm's famous nightlife district Stureplan throngs on Fridays and Saturdays, and the bohemian pubs and bars of Södermalm fill with revellers.

Festivals are celebrated with zest in Sweden. In cities, towns and villages, people come together to light bonfires on Walpurgis night, welcoming spring after the dark days of winter; they paint their children's faces and dress them up as witches for Easter; dance round the midsummer maypole; don silly hats and slurp crayfish claws in August; and revel in the lovely candlelit celebration of Lucia in December.

JAG ÄLSKAR SVERIGE (I LOVE SWEDEN)

No doubt some of this whole-hearted participation stems from an unshakeable faith in the rightness of Swedish ways. This attitude can irk its Scandinavian neighbours; but perhaps the Swedes' sense of satisfaction is not so misplaced. After all, Swedish exports are visible in all corners of the world, from retail giants such as H&M and IKEA, fashion brands like Acne Jeans to crime writers and mini television series.

A BRIEF HISTORY

Sweden has had a long and often turbulent history, with periods of economic and political superiority contrasting with a more recent decline in international importance. Constant throughout has been the relationship Swedes have with the sea: from the Baltic and North Seas to the inland waterways, it is this, more than anything, that has shaped the nation's history. No more so than with the Vikings, who swept into the world arena around AD800 in a fierce rush of longboats against an unguarded shore, killing and plundering as they went.

EARLY TIMES

Such is the conventional view, but Scandinavia actually reaches back 12,000 years to when the last Ice Age retreated. A basin of glaciers and sea was left behind and by 2000BC, the shape of the peninsula was much as it is today. Primitive hunters who had pushed north in the wake of the melting ice turned to farming and fishing.

A Viking memorial at Birka

During the Iron Age, independent tribes settled around the country, which came to be known as *Sverige*, or 'Land of the Svear', after the tribe on the shores of Lake Mälaren. Traces of these early Swedes are found all around the lake.

The vast majority of the Swedish Vikings went east rather than west. Their reasons for sailing were complex, but foremost in their minds were certainly thoughts of exploration, trade and conquest. They sailed deep into what is now Russia, spreading southeast as far as Constantinople, where some joined the Imperial Guard.

Much information about the early Svear has come to light through excavations at Birka, Sweden's first town. At its height (in AD800–960), Birka was the trading centre for a lakeside population of some 40,000 people, and now many graves and archaeological remains are dotted around Mälaren's shores. The Vikings are also recalled in tall rune stones decorated with a script that has long been decipherable. These are mostly in the Uppland region, just north of Stockholm, but one has been found as far north as Östersjön in Jämtland.

The Golden Room at Kalmar Slott

THE MIDDLE AGES

Christianity did not so much march into Sweden as slip in cautiously. In the 9th century, the Frankish monk St Ansgar was allowed to preach to the people of Birka, and around AD1000, Olof Skötkonung, the first Christian king of the Swedes, was baptised into the Byzantine Church, but failed to attract the Swedes to the new religion. In the mid-12th century, the pretender king Erik Jedvardsson (Erik IX, later St Erik, patron saint of the Swedes) was converted to Christianity, but only hesitantly did the Swedes give up the fierce paganism instilled by the Vikings.

Runes and rune stones

Viking rune stones had their heyday in the 10th century, but runic alphabets were used in Sweden from at least the 4th century, surviving to the 18th century in some parts of Dalarna.

Another strong medieval influence on Sweden was the German trading society (the Hanseatic League, or Hansa), which controlled trade in most of northern Europe. The Hansa was well rooted in Sweden, particularly on the island of Gotland, and enjoyed good trade between the Baltic and Germany.

In the 13th century, Sweden was taking control of what later became Finland, and there were alternating periods of harmony and strife with Denmark. In 1397, Denmark, under the rule of Queen Margareta, united Denmark, Norway and Sweden by way of the Kalmar Union.

Although Denmark and Norway were to remain united until 1814, Sweden's membership did not last much longer than a stormy century. The country withdrew in 1523, with the accession to the Swedish throne of Gustavus I (Gustav Vasa).

The Kalmar Union brought to the fore Swedish men such as Engelbrekt Engelbrektsson, a minor noble who led a rebellion against Danish taxes in 1434, as well as Sten Sture, who changed the course of Swedish history by defeating the Danish King Christian I at the Battle of Brunkeberg in 1471.

During its last 50 years, the Kalmar Union was anything but united, ending with the infamous Stockholm Bloodbath of 1520, when the Danish King Christian II executed 82 of Sweden's greatest citizens in Stockholm's Stortorget.

Gustav II Adolf

THE ROYAL DYNASTIES

From the early 15th century until the beginning of the 20th century, Sweden's history can be neatly divided into periods under different royal houses.

Gustav Vasa had just returned from exile when his father and nephew were killed in the Stockholm Bloodbath. Gustav raised a peasant army in Dalarna, which marched implacably southwards, capturing Danish strongholds along the route. Gustav was elected king on 6 June 1523 (celebrated throughout Sweden now as National Day), and the last bit of Danish opposition crumbled – 11 days later, the rebels entered Stockholm.

Gustav Vasa was a superb administrator and politician as well as a warrior. He harnessed the Hansa and reduced its power, cleverly manoeuvred the warring nobles and rich farmers, suppressed uprisings, and in 1527 implemented the Reformation, seizing control of the Church's lands and breaking up its power and wealth over the next 15 years. (The first Swedish Bible appeared in 1541.) His aim was less religious than financial, for, like King Henry VIII of England, he found the Church's riches very useful. (Monuments built by Gustav Vasa include the fortress-palaces at Vadstena, Uppsala and Gripsholm.)

His grandson, Gustav II Adolf, proved to be yet another brilliant warrior-statesman. During the Thirty Years' War, he crossed over the Baltic so successfully to fight against Livonia (Estonia and Latvia), Russia and Poland that it became known as 'the Swedish Pond'. At home, he left affairs in the capable hands of his excellent Chancellor, Axel Oxenstierna, who owned Tidö Slott on Lake Mälaren's south side.

King Gustav II Adolf was one of Sweden's greatest military geniuses, and might have brought even more changes to the map of Europe had he not been killed during the Thirty Years' War. He died at the age of 38 at the Battle of Lützen in 1632, in which Sweden beat the forces of the Holy Roman Empire. Like Gustav Vasa, he did much to open up Sweden, creating new towns, many in the north, such as Umeå and Luleå, and his greatest memorial, Gothenburg.

King Gustav II Adolf was succeeded by his daughter, Kristina, a child at the time, who abdicated in 1654 in favour of her cousin, Karl X. In him the Vasa dynasty's military genius

QUEEN KRISTINA

The warrior king, Gustav II Adolf, raised his daughter Kristina as he would have a son. One commentator wrote: 'Science is to Kristina what needle and cotton are to other women.' She was only six when her father died at Lützen, and she inherited the throne with the advantage of Gustav's formidable Chancellor, Axel Oxenstierna, as Regent.

Around the age of 16 Kristina began to attend her Council's meetings, and by the time she became queen in 1644 she well understood the ways of government. She presided over a sumptuous Baroque court filled with brilliant young minds that could match hers in knowledge and wit, but later grew bored with her role as queen and quarrelled with her Chancellor. One possible reason for her abdication in 1654 was her increasing sympathy with the Roman Catholic faith, coupled with her reluctance to marry. She travelled to Rome, where she shocked her former subjects by announcing her conversion. Her response was: 'Men can never admire, never approve a deed which they themselves are incapable of performing.'

flared again, albeit briefly, when he attacked Denmark in 1658 in a daring raid over the ice, forcing the Danes to hand over what are now Skåne, Halland, Blekinge and Gotland.

In 1697, the boy-king Karl XII inherited a strong kingdom with many overseas possessions, but also a legacy of war. Indeed, the Swedes look on Karl XII as a romantic military hero. In reality, however, after storming across Europe successfully, his army was very nearly wiped out by the Russians under Peter the Great in 1709 at the Battle of Poltava in Ukraine. The 50,000-strong Russian army slaughtered the 20,000 Swedes, leaving only 1,500 to flee south to Turkey with the king. Karl spent five years in Turkey and then, in a 15-day test of endurance, rode for 2,100km (1,300 miles) across Europe to return to Scandinavia. He was killed while fighting the Norwegians at Fredriksten Fortress in Norway, just over the border from Bohuslän in 1718. He had not set foot in his capital city in 18 years, and his death ended not only the Vasa dynasty but Sweden's era as a great European power.

FREEDOM AND ENLIGHTENMENT

This was the beginning, however, of a great age of freedom, with the transfer of power from the monarch to the Riksdag (parliament). A Swedish talent for invention also emerged, leading to the practical industrial developments of the late 19th and early 20th centuries. Botanist Carl von Linné (Linnaeus, 1707–78) published his definitive system for classifying plants, astronomer Anders Celsius (1701–44) invented the 100-degree temperature scale, and there were several successful chemists, including C.W. Scheele (1742–86), the first person to discover oxygen.

Liberty did not last long. Gustav III ascended the throne in 1771 and moved steadily towards absolutism and autocratic rule. However, he founded a native Swedish culture – indeed, his rule fell within the period known as the

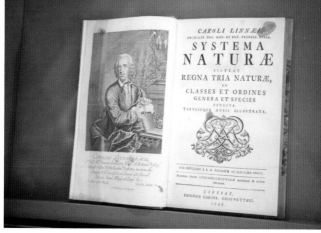

In the museum at the Linnaeus Garden, Uppsala

Gustavian Enlightenment. He built Stockholm's Royal Opera House and Royal Dramatic Theatre, and turned the theatre at Drottningholm Court into a showcase for Swedish talent.

King Gustav III was a fine writer himself, and attracted men of letters to the Court by founding the Swedish Academies of Literature, Music, Art, and History and Antiquities. However, the king could not ignore the wars with Russia that rumbled on periodically right up to the 19th century. Nor could his growing autocracy fail to disturb noble families, who felt their power slipping away to Gustav's more pliable favourites. The nobles plotted, and Gustav was assassinated at a masked opera ball – inspiring Verdi's opera *Un Ballo in Maschera*.

THE MAKING OF MODERN SWEDEN

As the Gustavian era faded away, the first decade of the 19th century was marked by several great changes in agriculture, constitution, foreign policy and, most noticeably at the time, dynasty. In 1810 the Riksdag, now with a written Constitution,

The Stadshuset (City Hall) in Stockholm

invited a French marshal in Napoleon's army, Jean-Baptiste Bernadotte, to become Crown Prince. It was a strange choice, particularly since Bernadotte had at one time headed an army waiting in Denmark to invade Sweden, but it proved justified. A firm hand was needed and the Swedes – who did not have confidence in Frederik VI of Denmark, the other main candidate for the position – found Bernadotte resolute in tackling the aftermath of the years of internal unrest.

In 1809 Sweden's long struggle with Russia came to an end, with the surrendering of Finland – a third of Sweden's territory – to Czar Alexander. Sweden then devoted the second half of the 19th century to internal development, with a late Industrial Revolution, using its natural assets in mining, saw-milling and the manufacturing of wood pulp, and promoting its successes in the inventive field, such as Alfred Nobel's dynamite and Gustaf Pasch's safety match. There was progress with the arrival of the co-operative movement, trade unionism and stirrings of the social democratic and women's movements.

Political problems still demanded attention. In 1814 the Danes ceded Norway to Sweden, but the Norwegians objected and set up their own independent parliament. As a compromise, in 1818 the Crown Prince was crowned King Karl XIV Johan of Sweden–Norway. He was wise enough to rule gently, but a growing sense of national identity and a cultural renaissance led Norway along the road to statehood. Friction increased between the two countries until, in 1905, the union between Sweden and Norway came to an end.

In addition, a mounting agricultural crisis in the 1880s led to the emigration of what was eventually to be a total of more than one million people by the 1930s. So many Swedes settled in North America that some communities in Minnesota and Wisconsin subsequently spoke only Swedish for at least one generation. Today, thousands of these pioneers' descendants return to Sweden to visit their roots every year.

THE 20TH CENTURY AND BEYOND

Despite the successes of the 19th century – including the establishment of a railway network, universal education and a good supply of raw materials – Sweden entered the 20th century a poor country, with 80 percent of the population involved in rural industries. The Industrial Revolution brought poverty at first, but industrialisation took hold rapidly and during World War I the demand for Swedish products brought new hope. Yet no sooner were things picking up than the Great Depression hit Sweden and the country was plagued by widespread unemployment. Strikes took place, leading to a tragic incident in 1931 in which soldiers opened fire on demonstrators from Ångermanland, injuring many and killing five.

Political changes happened gradually, without bloodshed; the introduction of universal suffrage in 1921 led to a system of elections, political parties and a democratic government.

Head of state, King Carl XVI Gustaf, and Queen Silvia

In the early 1900s, the monarchy found itself under pressure, with calls for the abdication of Gustav V. The king rode the storm, however, and emerged as a popular ruler after World War I. His great-grandson, the present King, Carl XVI Gustav, has endeavoured to ensure the monarchy's wellbeing, although the publication of a scandalous biography in 2010 rocked the boat.

The 20th century was also a period of social democracy and national neutrality, with Sweden refusing to take part in either world war, though the country has since been active in the United Nations. The Social Democrats were in power for most of the 70 years preceding 2006, although differences between left and right have often been softened by consensus politics. Even the tragic, and still-unexplained, assassination of the Social Democratic Prime Minister, Olof Palme, in 1986, did not lead to further instability, though his death did shake the nation's confidence.

Sweden joined the European Union in 1995, but rejected the euro in 1999 and again in a 2003 referendum. In recent years, there has been an ongoing shift from a socialist underpinning of the economy towards a more liberal free-market approach. In 2006 the centre-right coalition Alliansen came to power, ousted in 2014 by the Social Democrats. Far-right, anti-immigration groups have also made political headway in an uncertain economic climate.

HISTORICAL LANDMARKS

c. AD94 Roman historian Tacitus mentions *Svear*.

8th–11th centuries Swedish Vikings range through Russia as far as Constantinople.

c. 790 Birka established as a trading post.

829–31 Ansgar tries to introduce Christianity.

993–1024 Reign of Olof Skötkonung, first Christian king of Sweden.

12th century Hanseatic League begins to dominate trade.

1397 Denmark, Sweden and Norway united.

1435 Meeting of the first Riksdag (parliament).

1520 Stockholm Bloodbath.

1523 Gustav Vasa elected king; founds the Swedish nation state and the Vasa dynasty.

1527 Gustav Vasa imposes Reformation.

1718 Karl XII killed and Vasa dynasty ends.

1718–71 Age of Freedom; Riksdag gains in power.

18th century Gustav III promotes culture and arts.

1808–9 Sweden loses Finland to Russia.

1814 Danes cede Norway to Sweden.

1818 Crown Prince becomes King Karl XIV Johan of Sweden–Norway.

1880s–90s Industrial Revolution begins. Agricultural crisis leads to mass Swedish emigration.

1905 Norway gains independence.

1914–18 World War I; Sweden remains neutral.

1939–45 World War II; Sweden declares neutrality.

1986 Prime Minister Olof Palme assassinated.

1995 Sweden joins European Union.

2000 Church separates from state after 400 years.

2003 Foreign Minister Anna Lindh murdered. Swedes reject the euro in national referendum.

2011 Swede's carry out world's first synthetic organ transplant.

2015 A complete overhaul of Swedish money begins, with newly-designed banknotes and the introduction of the new denomination of 200-krona.

WHERE TO GO

Don't underestimate Sweden's size. It is the third-largest country in Western Europe, and with an average of only 23 people per square kilometre, there are often long stretches of empty countryside between towns and it's definitely easier to visit the country by a region at a time.

In this guide Sweden is divided into six main regions, each of which is subdivided according to old provincial names. These may not coincide with local government regions, but they are the names used by the Swedes themselves.

STOCKHOLM

The Swedish capital **Stockholm** ❶ is a city floating on 14 islands between sea and lake. Everywhere trees, gardens and buildings are never far from a harbour or shore. At a time when water provided the easiest transport route, the small settlement where Lake Mälaren in the west gave way to the eastern Baltic Sea became the natural gateway to inland Sweden.

Today, salt and freshwater are divided by the heavy lock gates of Slussen. Big Baltic ferries wait at the quays, and, in summer, boats scurry over the sparkling surface. Remarkably, this water is as clean as it looks, and you can swim and fish for salmon right in the city centre.

The heart of the city is very compact, and best covered either on foot, or, as an introduction, by sightseeing boat tours from Stadhuskajen. The main areas are Gamla Stan (the medieval Old Town); Norrmalm, the modern business centre; Östermalm, with up-market shops and affluent houses; Djurgården, an outdoor playground; and Södermalm, a bohemian bit of town. Pleasant suburbs stretch along the water to the west and east, housing a significant portion of Greater

Sunset at the Bohuslän Coast

Stockholm's population of around 2.2 million (only 920,000 live in the city itself).

GAMLA STAN

In Gamla Stan (Old Town), Stockholm's history dates back more than seven centuries. Cross by the Riksbron (bridge) and your route will take you literally through the Swedish **Riksdagshuset**, the House of Parliament (www.riksdagen. se; guided tours late June–Aug Mon–Fri noon, 1pm, 2pm and 3pm, Oct–early June Sat–Sun 1.30pm; free). During reconstruction work on the Riksdagshuset, a medieval churchyard and city walls were unearthed, and these now form the core of the excellent **Medeltidsmuseet** (Medieval Museum; www. medeltidsmuseet.stockholm.se; daily Tue–Sun noon–5pm, Wed until 8pm; free), hidden away underneath the bridge.

Just beyond the Riksdag is **Kungliga Slottet Ⓐ** (Royal Palace; www.kungahuset.se; mid-May–mid-Sept daily 10am–5pm, mid-Sept–mid-May Tue–Sun 10am–4pm), containing over 600 rooms and three museums. The present building was erected on the site of Tre Kronor (Three Crowns)

A NEW VIEW

It's always fun to see Stockholm from a different angle. Explore it at water level in a **kayak** or **paddle boat** from Djurgårdsbron Sjöcafe (www.sjocafeet.se). Alternatively (vertigo sufferers, look away), popular **rooftop tours** (www.takvandring.com) take you up among the gables of Riddarholmen. The Stadsmuseet's **Millennium tour** (see page 35) follows the footsteps of *The Girl with the Dragon Tattoo*. Underground, Stockholm's metro system is described as 'the world's longest art gallery': download a free Art Guide from the website of the city's transport provider, SL (http://sl.se).

Palace, which burned down in 1697 when the palace fire wardens neglected their duty. Nicodemus Tessin the Younger drew up the plans for the building that stands today. The Apartments of State and other rooms with magnificent interiors are open to the public, including **Oscar II's Writing Room**, full of 19th-century furniture and

Inside the Kungliga Slottet

unaltered since the king's death in 1907. Down in the cellars are the **Crown Jewels**, beautifully lit and displayed in the **Skattkammaren** (Royal Treasury). The Royal Guard parades down Norrmalm's Hamngatan, and over the bridge to the palace for the **Changing of the Guard** (May–Aug Mon–Sat 12.15pm, Sun and holidays 1.15pm, see website www.forsvars makten.se for other months).

Also below the palace is the **Royal Armoury** (Livrust- kammaren; http://livrustkammaren.se; July–Aug daily 10am–6pm, May daily 11am–5pm, June daily 10am–5pm, Jan–Apr and Sept–Dec Tue–Wed and Fri–Sun 11am–5pm, Thu 11am–8pm; Thu after 5pm free), containing gems such as the stuffed horse of the renowned warrior king Gustav II Adolf. Right next to the palace is the **Storkyrkan** (Great Cathedral; daily 9am–4pm), a high-ceilinged Gothic building and Stockholm's oldest, dating from around 1279. Used as a parish church and for ceremonial occasions, it holds the famous statue of **St George and the Dragon**, a large wood-carving by Bernt Notke from 1489. The nearby **Tyska Kyrkan** (German Church), with its spiky green tower, is almost as old, a reminder of the medieval German traders.

The Storkyrkan

At any time, people throng the shopping streets of Västerlånggatan and Österlånggatan. This is a good area to wander around. Visit **Mårten Trotzigs Gränd**, the narrowest street of all, at the southern end of Västerlånggatan; more a stairway than a lane, it is a mere 90cm (35 inches) wide at its narrowest point.

At the centre of this tangle of streets is **Stortorget**, the square in which 82 Swedes were killed in the Stockholm Bloodbath. On one side is **Börsen**, the former Stock Exchange, home to the interesting **Nobelmuseet** (www.nobelmuseum.se; June–Aug daily 10am–8pm, Sept–May Tue 11am–8pm and Wed–Sun 11am–5pm), which documents the history of the Nobel Prize.

On the western side of Gamla Stan, in a square called Riddarhustorget, is the 17th-century **Riddarhuset** (House of Nobility; www.riddarhuset.se; Mon–Fri 11am–noon), Stockholm's most beautiful building, with its interior distinguished by 2,326 noble coats of arms. Over a bridge farther west is **Riddarholmen** (Island of the Nobles), with the distinctive latticework spire of the 700-year-old **Riddarholmskyrkan** (Church of the Nobility), where all the nation's monarchs since Gustav II Adolf have been laid to rest in sarcophagi.

NORRMALM

Many older buildings were replaced by modern blocks during the 1960s, and Norrmalm became all the poorer for it. The demolition process was stopped, however, when Stockholmers rebelled and climbed the trees in **Kungsträdgården**, a pleasant square off Hamngatan, defying the men bulldozing the area. Thanks to them, the King's Garden park remains the open-air heart of Norrmalm, home to summer festivals and a small ice-skating rink in winter.

A memorial to the period of demolition is **Sergels Torg**, a huge square with a giant glass obelisk at the top of Hamngatan. Opposite is the **Kulturhuset** (www.kulturhuset. stockholm.se), a modern cultural centre where thousands meet daily to see exhibitions, watch films or enjoy a fine view of the city while drinking coffee at the Café Panorama.

For a taste of one of Stockholm's popular street markets, stroll along Sergelgatan past the glass skyscrapers to **Hötorget**, a typical, colourful fruit, flower and vegetable market. Here, too, is the **Konserthuset** (www.konserthuset.se), base of the Stockholm Philharmonic Orchestra and a venue for a variety of concerts, from classical to rock. In front of this fine building stands the lovely **Orpheus Fountain**, the work of famous sculptor Carl Milles.

To the west, Norrmalm ends at Tegelbacken, with a good view of the **Stadshuset** ⑧ (City Hall; www.stockholm.se/ stadshuset; English guided tours: around six daily, depending on municipal events; tower: daily, access every 40 minutes, May and Sept 9.15am–3.55pm, June–Aug 9.15am–5.15pm) on the next island, Kungsholmen. Its massive 105m (450ft) square

Online royalty

Visit www.kungahuset.se for detailed information on all the royal attractions in Sweden, including the Changing of the Guard at the Royal Palace.

Looking out over the Stadshuset

tower –offering tremendous views – is topped with the golden Tre Kronor (three crowns) that are the city's symbol. Popular tours (book ahead) allow you to see the fascinating interior, including the elegant Blue Hall where the Nobel Prize banquet is held. Boats for Mälaren depart from the quay below.

DJURGÅRDEN AND SKEPPSHOLMEN

Djurgården ('deer park') was once a royal hunting ground and has retained much of its rural feel. Together with neighbouring Skeppsholmen, it contains some of Stockholm's best museums and attractions. You can reach the islands by bridge, or better still take the ferry from Nybroviken or Slussen, giving you the chance to admire the bustling harbour and its myriad small boats from the water.

Skeppsholmen is the permanent home for the **Moderna Museet ⓒ** (www.modernamuseet.se; Tue and Fri 10am–8pm, Wed–Thu and Sat–Sun 10am–6pm), housing an art collection that includes works by Picasso, Braque, Léger, Dali and

Kandinsky. The **ArkDes** (the Swedish Centre for Architecture and Design; www.arkdes.se; Tue 10am–8pm, Wed–Sun 10am–6pm), with the same entrance as the Moderna Museet, guides visitors through 1,000 years of Scandinavian building. Nearby is the **Östasiatiska Museet** (Museum of Asian Art; www.ostasiatiska.se; Tue–Sun 11am–5pm), in a former royal stables. The museum's exhibitions include a fine collection of Chinese art once belonging to King Gustav VI Adolf. Just north of Skeppholmen (linked by bridge) is Blasieholmen. Here you'll find the **Nationalmuseum** (www.nationalmuseum. se; closed for renovation until 2018), with artworks by 16th- to 20th-century European masters and by the great Swedish painters, Anders Zorn and Carl Larsson.

As the ferry nears Djurgården, the screams of roller-coaster-riders meet your ears. **Gröna Lund** ⓓ (www.grona lund.com; June–Aug daily, May and Sept Thu–Sun, see website for hours), a compact little 19th-century amusement park, has some fun rides and a prime waterside setting. For the more discerning visitor, however, Djurgården means the Vasa and Skansen museums.

The 17th-century **Vasa warship** was built as the pride of the fleet for Gustav II Adolf, but, unfortunately, pride did indeed come before a fall. Top-heavy from the weight of her guns and ornate decoration, the *Vasa* sank on her maiden voyage before horrified crowds who had turned out for the occasion. Rediscovered in the 1950s by a determined marine

---

Tourist office

Stockholm Visitor Centre (www.visitstockholm.com; open daily year-round), located in Kulturhuset at Sergels Torg 5, provides maps and guides, and can help you to book accommodation and tours in Stockholm and surrounding areas. Tickets for theatre, concerts and sports events, as well as the Stockholm Pass (see page 117), can be purchased here.

archaeologist, Anders Franzén, the ship has been returned to her former glory. Today, in the state-of-the-art **Vasamuseet ⓔ** (www.vasamuseet.se; daily 10am–5pm, Wed until 8pm), the *Vasa* is a magnificent sight, with 'cutaway' floors showing the structure from keel to decks.

The oldest open-air museum in the world, **Skansen ⓕ** (www.skansen.se; tel: 08-442 80 00; open from 10am daily – closing times vary), contains 150 quaint old Swedish buildings, populated by working craftspeople in summer. Skansen's zoo contains Scandinavian creatures: bears, wolves and reindeer.

This island playground also boasts the worthwhile **Nordiska Museet** (www.nordiskamuseet.se; daily 10am–5pm; Sept–May Wed until 8pm, free after 5pm), which explains Nordic life from the 16th century onwards, and the **Thielska Galleriet** (www. thielska-galleriet.se; Tue–Sun noon–5pm, Thu until 8pm), the collection of a 19th-century Stockholm banker who hobnobbed

The magnificent Vasamuseet

with Sweden's finest artists. The newest addition to the area is **ABBA the Museum** (www.abbathemuseum.com; daily 10am–6pm), an interactive musuem that plays tribute to Sweden's most popular band. The exquisite gallery **Prins Eugens Waldemarsudde** (www.waldemarsudde.com; Tue–Sun 11am–5pm, Thu until 8pm), former home of the so-called 'painter prince' Eugén, has lovely gardens and sea views.

Slussen

The redevelopment of Slussen – a major transport hub in Stockholm – is due to be completed by 2022. Expect disruption as the city authorities replace the old Slussen lock and adjoining roads with a totally revamped waterfront, designed by Norman Foster. The completed works will include a new park, plaza, retail space, boat docks, bus terminal and cycle lanes.

A short walk across the bridge in the Östermalm area is the **Historiska Museet** (www.historiska.se; June–Aug daily 10am–6pm, Sept–May Tue–Sun 11am–5pm, Wed until 8pm). The highlight is the spectacular Guldrummet (Gold Room), containing over 3,000 prehistoric gold and silver artefacts.

SÖDERMALM

Commonly referred to as 'Söder', this was once the great working-class area of Stockholm. Today it is the most bohemian part of town: the steep street Hornsgatan is filled with galleries and craft shops, while the 'SoFo' area (south of Folkungagatan) contains the coolest cafés and bars.

Södermalm forms the backdrop to much of Stieg Larsson's bestselling Millennium Trilogy (*The Girl With the Dragon Tattoo* and follow-ups). Although the **Stadsmuseum** (City Museum; www.stadsmuseum.stockholm.se) is closed for renovation until autumn 2017, it still runs popular walking tours: the Millennium Tour and ABBA City Walk. Afterwards, you may take a trip to

The state bedchamber at Drottningholm Palace

one of the city's most curious sights: **Katarinahissen**, a historic lift that until 2010 used to carry passengers to the heights of Södermalm (it should reopen at the turn of the decade following major redevelopment of Slussen).

The fabulous new **Fotografiska** ⑤ exhibition hall (http://fotografiska.eu; daily 10am–11pm) showcases four major photographic exhibitions every year. So far, the superb spaces of this former Customs House have featured everything from a Robert Mapplethorpe retrospective to contemporary reportage.

LAKE MÄLAREN AND THE ARCHIPELAGO

Lake Mälaren stretches 100km (62 miles) west of Stockholm and has innumerable enticing islands. A good day out is by vintage steamer to Drottningholm on Lovön (some 50 minutes from Stadshuskajen).

Lovön has long been a royal island. The Unesco World Heritage Site **Drottningholm Palace** ❷ (www.kungahuset. se; Apr daily 11am–3.30pm, May–Sept daily 10am–4.30pm, Oct Fri–Sun 11am–3.30pm, Nov–Dec and Jan–Mar Sat–Sun noon–3.30pm; gardens free), built in the 17th century and now the royal family's main home, draws comparisons with Versailles. A large portion of the palace is open to the public. Most popular is **Drottningholm Court Theatre** (www.dtm.se;

guided tours Apr daily 11am–3.30pm, May–Aug daily 11am–4.30pm, Sept daily noon–3pm, Oct Sun noon–3.30pm, Nov–Dec Sat–Sun noon–3.30pm), built in 1766 by Queen Lovisa Ulrika to entertain the Royal Court. Gustav III inherited his mother's passion for the arts; but after his assassination at a masked ball, the theatre was shut and forgotten until the 1920s, when Professor Agne Beijer pushed open the door and found it perfectly preserved down to the last detail. Opera and ballet are performed here in the summer and guided tours show the original backdrops and equipment.

The palace's other show-stopper is the ornate **Kina Slott** (Chinese Pavilion; daily May–Aug 11am–4.30pm, Sept noon–3.30pm), originally a birthday present for lucky Lovisa Ulrika.

Farther west, on the island of **Björkö**, is another Unesco World Heritage Site. The Viking town of **Birka ❸**, Sweden's oldest settlement (founded c.790), was a thriving trading centre of 40,000 people in its prime. In those days, nothing divided Lake Mälaren from the Baltic Sea, and travellers, traders and even an early Christian missionary sailed straight in from Europe, Russia and Arabia. Today there's a small museum and costumed re-enactors in summer; and you can take a guided tour around the 3,000 Viking grave mounds and excavation sites (www.raa.se).

East of Stockholm's city centre are the inner islands of the archipelago, best seen on an excursion that lasts about seven hours. Water sets the mood for **Millesgården ❹** (www.millesgarden.se; May–Sept daily 11am–5pm,

Ferry services

The ferry companies Waxholmsbolaget (tel: 08-600 10 00; www.waxholmsbolaget.se) and Strömma (tel: 08-1200 40 00; www.stromma.se) offer a variety of cruises and scheduled crossings to destinations in the Archipelago. Waxholm boats sail from Strömkajen, by the Grand Hotel, and Strömma boats depart from Strandvägen, Nybroplan or Stadshusbron.

Oct–Apr Tue–Sun 11am–5pm), the summer home of sculptor Carl Milles (1875–1955), on **Lidingö**. Here he reproduced the statues that had made him famous. Set on steep terraces, the figures seem to fly, as if defying gravity.

Vaxholm is a great place for water sports. The **Fortress**, housing the **Fästnings Museet** (Fortress Museum; www.vaxholmsfastning.se), dates from the 16th century and was built to guard Stockholm's main sea route. Vaxholm now has more peaceful purposes, with waterside paths and plenty of idyllic houses, cafés and restaurants.

STOCKHOLM'S SURROUNDINGS

UPPSALA

Sweden's ancient capital **Uppsala** lies 70km (44 miles) north of Stockholm. **Gamla Uppsala ⑤** (Old Uppsala), 5km (3 miles) north of the modern centre, was an Iron Age pagan stronghold. Three huge grave mounds dominate the fields around **Gamla Uppsala Museum** (www.raa.se; Apr–Sept daily 11am–5pm;Oct–Dec and Jan–Mar Mon, Wed, Sat–Sun noon–4pm), which does a good job of explaining these enigmatic Viking remains.

Christianity finally overcame Uppsala in the 12th century, and is still going strong: the town boasts Scandinavia's largest Gothic cathedral, **Uppsala Domkyrka** (daily 8am–6pm). Here, too, is Sweden's oldest **university**, which ensures a lively student contingent around the narrow streets. The **Gustavianum** (www.gustavianum.uu.se; Tue–Sun 11am–4pm) is a fascinating collection of historical bits and bobs, topped by a 17th-century anatomical theatre where students watched operations being performed.

Famous alumni of the university include Carl von Linné (Linnaeus), the botanist who devised the modern method of animal and plant classification. **Linnéträdgården** (www.linnaeus.

uu.se; May and Sept Tue–Sun 11am–8pm, June–Aug daily 11am–8pm, museum until 5pm) is an interesting reconstruction of his 18th-century garden, although Uppsala's **botanical gardens** are better for summer strolling.

The city is dominated by its castle, **Uppsala Slott** (www. uppsalaslott.com; guided tours in English July–Aug Tue–Sun 1pm and 3pm). This brick fortress is where Gustav II Adolf held talks that plunged Sweden into the Thirty Years' War, and where Queen Kristina gave up her crown.

Inside Uppsala Domkyrka

Off the E4 route to Uppsala from Stockholm is **Sigtuna**, thought to be Sweden's oldest existing town, with a pretty medieval main street. Further north, in a cluster of lakes, is splendid **Skokloster** (http://skoklostersslott. se; June–Aug daily 11am–5pm, May and Sept Sat–Sun 11am–4pm), a 17th-century castle commissioned by the powerful Wrangel family, but never completed due to its owner's death. Everything is as it was on the day the builders downed tools.

AROUND LAKE MÄLAREN

Leaving Stockholm on the E20/E4 on Mälaren's southern side, the first stop is the idyllic small town of **Mariefred** – which can also be reached by steamship from Stadhuskajen. This is a typical lakeside town and site of the 16th-century castle **Gripsholm Slott** (www.kungahuset.se; mid-May–Sept daily 10am–4pm,

At Gripsholm Slott

mid-Apr–mid-May and Oct–Nov Sat–Sun noon–3pm), once owned by Gustav Vasa. Gripsholm's royal portraits are compelling, and a small theatre goes back to the days of that royal patron of the arts, Gustav III. Another delight is the **Östra Södermanlands Järnväg** (East Södermanland Railway; www.oslj.nu), a superb steam railway between Mariefred and Läggesta, 4km (2.5 miles) away.

West from Gripsholm, the pretty little town of **Strängnäs** holds a vast **Gothic Cathedral**. Follow meandering back roads further west: 17th-century **Sundbyholms Slott** (www.sundbyholms-slott.se) is now a hotel and restaurant, from where **Sigurdsristningen**, an unusual Viking-era rock carving, is a short walk through the beech woods.

Eskilstuna has a strong iron-working past and several industrial museums, although today it's better known for its family-friendly **Parken Zoo** (www.parkenzoo.se; May–Sept daily 10am–5pm, July until 7pm), with a pride of white tigers and funfair rides.

At the western end of the lake, **Arboga** has some of the best-preserved buildings in Sweden. In 1435 this town was the meeting place for what later became Sweden's first Riksdag (parliament) and for the election of Engelbrekt Engelbrektsson to the position of Captain of the Realm.

On the northwestern shore is a banana-yellow Baroque palace, **Strömsholms Slott** (www.kungahuset.se; June–Aug daily noon–4pm, July until 5pm), once a royal residence. There is an excellent riding centre with a carriage museum here. Watersports enthusiasts should head towards **Kolbäcksån** and, close by, the **Strömsholm Canal**.

Heading east on the E18 you come to **Västerås**, an early trade centre, with a **cathedral** that holds the tomb of Erik XIV. Västerås is also a pleasure-sailing centre linked to the capital by ferry. Not far away, **Anundshög** has Sweden's largest Iron Age burial mounds and ship tumuli.

South of Västerås, the 17th-century **Tidö Slott** (www.tidoslott. se; July–mid-Aug Tue–Sun noon–5pm, May and June Sat–Sun noon–5pm) was the home of Axel Oxenstierna, the great Swedish Regent who ruled during the childhood of Gustav II's daughter, Kristina. Today, Tidö houses a **Toy Museum** with some 35,000 items, and the grounds are home to hundreds of deer.

Before heading back to Stockholm, take a detour to the ancient estate of **Engsö Slott** (http://engso.se; July–mid-Aug Tue–Sun noon–4pm, May–June and 2nd half of Aug Sat–Sun noon–4pm), full of legends, on its own island of **Ängsö** – a good place for swimming, fishing, canoeing, walking and camping.

THE SOUTH

The south of Sweden between the Kattegatt and the Baltic seas has a character shaped by both history and proximity to Continental Europe. The area is also mellowed by a warmer climate than most of the rest of the country and is made more cosmopolitan by its role as a summer playground.

SKÅNE

Thanks to its fertility, Skåne is known as 'Sweden's Granary'. It was a prize that Sweden and Denmark fought over for

Ales Stenar

'Scandinavia's Stonehenge', built around 1,400 years ago, lies 10km (6 miles) from Ystad. Its 59 hefty sandstone boulders are arranged in a ship-like formation; some of them were transported to the site from 20km (12 miles) away.

centuries: the accent still has a hint of Danish. Today, relations are far more friendly, with hundreds of passengers sailing every day between Helsingborg (Sweden) and Helsingør (Denmark).

Skåne has Sweden's most prosperous farms, set in a landscape of rich colour. The magnificent coastline offers beaches, fishing villages, skerries for sea-fishing, and, on the **Bjäre Peninsula** to the northwest, rocks shaped like statues at **Hovs hallar**.

The South's long-established wealth is reflected in more than 250 castles and historic buildings. Standing on an island in Lake Ringsjön is **Bosjökloster** (www.bosjokloster.se; May–Sept 10am–5pm; gardens year-round). Dating from about 1080, this former Benedictine convent has a fine 12th-century church, beautiful gardens containing a thousand-year-old oak tree, and a small zoo. In addition, many towns are fortified – Helsingborg, dominated by its medieval keep, **Kärnan**; and **Landskrona**, farther south, with a **Citadellet** (www.citadellet.com) dating from 1549.

On the southwestern tip of Skåne are summer resorts **Falsterbo** and **Skanör**, while fine scenery awaits you on the east coast. Ferry routes link workaday **Trelleborg**, on the south coast, to the German ports of Travemünde, Rostock and Sassnitz. Farther on, 13th-century **Ystad** – the setting for Henning Mankell's Inspector Wallander series – has many rare old houses in a near-Tudor style, and is the ferry departure point for the Danish isle of **Bornholm**. A few kilometres east are the enigmatic **Ales Stenar** ❻. One of Sweden's most visited national parks, **Stenshuvud**, rises majestically above the Baltic further along the coast.

Fifteenth-century **Glimmingehus** ❼ (www.raa.se; June–mid-Aug 10am–6pm, mid-Aug–Sep and Apr–May 11am–4pm), southwest of **Simrishamn**, is regarded by some as the best-preserved medieval fortress in Scandinavia – and allegedly the most haunted. As well as an on-site museum, during summer there are several guided tours daily.

MALMÖ AND LUND

Malmö ❽, Sweden's third-largest city and one of the world's most cycling-friendly, is a rare mixture of old and new, and is home to 310,000 residents from 177 different nations. At the heart of the city is the giant square, **Stortorget**, built in 1536 under the initiative of Jörgen Kock, Malmö's powerful mayor at the time. He was also responsible for the fine

The Malmö skyline is dominated by Turning Torso

Öresund Bridge

On the outskirts of Malmö, the 16km (10-mile) Öresund Bridge (http://oresundsbron.com) links Sweden to Denmark; many people living in Malmö now work in Copenhagen, bringing the two countries together like never before. Get a cup of coffee and marvel at the sight from Sundspromenaden, Västra Hamnen.

Rådhus (City Hall) and his private residence **Jörgen Kocks Hus**, one of the earliest private houses to be built in the city. Just off the square to the east is the lovely, 14th-century **St Petri's Kyrka**, replete with treasures from the 16th and 17th centuries. Danish King Kristian III built **Malmöhus Slott** when Skåne was still part of Denmark. Based in and around the castle today are the **Malmö Museer** (http://malmo.se/museer), a collection of museums focusing on art, local history, the sea and technology, along with an aquarium.

Built in 1592 as a market square, **Lilla Torg** is one of the most popular meeting places in the city. It has several interesting 16th-century buildings and is home to the **Form/Design Center** (www.formdesigncenter.com), which exhibits design and architecture. In the summer Lilla Torg is filled with outdoor restaurants and cafés and has a vibrant and enchanting atmosphere. Contemporary international artists are celebrated at both **Malmö Konsthall** (www.konsthall.malmo.se) and the **Moderna Museet Malmö** (www.modernamuseet.se; Tue–Sun 11am–6pm, Tue and Fri until 8pm; Fri after 6pm free), which threw open its doors in 2010.

In recent years, Malmö's Western Harbour (Västra Hamnen) has undergone ambitious redevelopment, symbolised by architect Santiago Calatrava's spectacular apartment building **Turning Torso**. At 190m (623ft), it is the tallest building in Sweden. New bars and restaurants and a long stretch of beach make this a popular spot in summer.

Malmö comes alive during August for the free, week-long **Malmö Festival** (www.malmofestivalen.se): a music, culinary and cultural festival combined.

Lund ❾, approximately 25km (15 miles) northeast of Malmö, is a gracious university city with winding, cobbled streets, old buildings and an atmosphere of age and learning. It is believed to have been founded in AD990 by Danish King Sven Tveskägg ('Fork beard'). In 1020 his son King Canute began to turn it into a political, cultural, commercial and religious centre. By 1103 it had become the seat of the Archbishop of all Scandinavia and Finland. Lund's towering Romanesque Cathedral, **Domkyrkan**, which was consecrated in 1145, has a fine altarpiece dating from the 15th century.

The university library in Lund

Lund University, founded in 1666, is set in beautiful gardens. Its 33,000 students form an important part of Lund's modest population of 120,000, and are particularly noticeable on such special occasions as Walpurgis night (see page 94).

Lund has good museums: worth visiting are the open-air museum **Kulturen** (www.kulturen.com; May–Aug daily 10am–5pm, Sept–Apr Tue–Sun noon–4pm); the subterranean **Drottens Museum** (Mon–Fri 10am–5pm, Sat 11am–5pm), with its medieval skeletons; **Skissernas Museum** (Museum of Sketches; www.adk.lu.se;

closed for development until autumn 2016), a collection of artists' preliminary studies and sketches; and the archaeological
Historiska Museet (www.luhm.lu.se; Tue–Fri 11am–4pm, Sun
noon–4pm; free).

BLEKINGE

The Swedish writer Selma Lagerlöf described Blekinge as the
land of three steps – coast, inland and forest. It has a string of
small towns with long histories, and its archipelago (Sweden's
most southerly) has countless islands. Inland, the forest once
acted as a refuge for outlaws from the border wars; it is dotted
with small, well-concealed villages. This miniature province is
in fact something of a microcosm of Sweden, right down to its
famous salmon river and good golf course.

Blekinge's largest town, 17th-century **Karlskrona ⑩**, is built
on 30 islands and has had a long association with the Swedish
Navy. Karl XI had the city constructed as a navy stronghold
against Denmark: its wide streets, old buildings and well-preserved fortresses have earned it a place on the Unesco World
Heritage List. It has excellent facilities for boating, fishing and
swimming. **Marinmuseum** (www.marinmuseum.se; June–Aug
daily 10am–6pm, May and Sept daily 10am–4pm, Oct–Apr Tue–
Sun 10am–4pm), which won the Swedish Museum of the Year
award in 2015, has a great collection of ships' figureheads.

On the E22 into Blekinge from Skåne in the west, small
towns are found mostly on the coast. The exception is **Olof-
ström**, 30km (21 miles) north on the Skåne border, nestled
among woods and water: **Lake Halen** is a particular beauty
spot, good for bathing and canoeing.

A number of Blekinge's coastal towns are worth a visit. In
medieval **Sölvesborg**, the ruins of **Sölvesborg Slott**, a castle from the 13th century, draw visitors, and **Mörrum** (on
the **Mörrumsån**, a superb salmon river) attracts anglers

from near and far. **Karlshamn** is notable for its **Emigrants' Monument**, a moving tribute to those who left their homes for a brave new world across the ocean.

SMÅLAND

Historically Småland's crofters lived off an ungrateful land of thick forests, interspersed with bogs and lakes. The province breeds tough, determined people: famous natives include tennis players Mats Wilander and Stefan Edberg, soprano Jenny Lind (the 'Swedish Nightingale') and writer Astrid Lindgren. Småland is also the birthplace of flat-pack-furniture giant IKEA, which plans to turn its first store in Älmhult into a fully-fledged museum (due to open in spring 2016).

The majority of the one million people who emigrated to America came from Småland; today many people return from the New World to trace their roots.

Kalmar Slott

Kalmar ⑪ is an ancient city, first noted on an 11th-century rune stone. It has a compelling history: the Kalmar Union was signed here in 1397, and the city was also one of the trading ports of the powerful German Hanseatic League. The formidable 16th-century **Kalmar Slott** (www.kalmarslott.se; May–Sept daily 10am–4pm, July–Aug until 6pm, Apr and Oct–Nov Sat–Sun 10am–4pm) guards the straits between the mainland and Öland, looking every inch a fairy-tale castle. Its founder, the mad king Erik XIV, commissioned some unusual features, including a secret escape tunnel through the royal privy.

In May 1676, during a skirmish against the Danish–Dutch fleet, Sweden suffered its biggest ever shipping disaster when the royal flagship *Kronan* turned too quickly, capsized and

A DARING RAID

Until 1658 the border between the provinces of Blekinge and Småland was Sweden's uneasy frontier with Denmark. Marked by the small community of Kristianopel, once a Danish fortress, the area was fought over for centuries. Then, the icy winter of 1657–8 gave Sweden's King Karl X Gustav his chance...

Arctic weather froze the sea between Sweden and Denmark and the Great Belt separating Denmark's first and second islands. Though already at war with Poland and Russia, Karl Gustav sent his troops onto the ice. Two squadrons of horses and riders fell through and drowned, but 5,000 foot soldiers and 1,500 cavalry reached Denmark's central island, Fyn.

Despite a thaw, they followed that journey with an even more hazardous crossing to Denmark's main island, Sjælland (Zealand), and reached the walls of Copenhagen. Denmark had no choice but to agree to the Treaty of Roskilde and cede its northern provinces on the mainland to Sweden. They have remained Swedish ever since.

was ripped apart by a massive explosion. Only 42 souls survived from an 850-strong crew. The ship was rediscovered in 1980, and 30,000 objects have now been retrieved. Treasures, including the ship's bell, bronze cannon, gold coins and some 300-year-old brandy, are displayed at the excellent **Kalmar Länsmuseum** (www.kalmar lansmuseum.se; Mon–Fri 10am–4pm, Sat–Sun 11am–6pm, until 8pm Wed).

At work in the Glasriket

The northern archipelago called the **Blue Coast**, where Småland shades into Östergötland, offers fishing villages, beaches and hundreds of islands and harbours for all kinds of water sports. **Västervik**, 130km (90 miles) north of Kalmar, an excellent starting point for deep-sea fishing, holds a **Visfestivalen** (Song Festival) in mid-July, attracting many of Sweden's top performers. Ferries to Gotland leave from Oskarshamn, to the south.

Heading inland on Highway 33 from Västervik will bring you to **Vimmerby**, birthplace of the much-loved children's writer Astrid Lindgren (1907–2002). You can visit her childhood home, **Astrid Lindgrens Näs** (www.astridlindgrensnas.se; mid-June–mid-Sept daily 10am–6pm, early May June–mid-June and mid-Sept daily 11am–4pm, Mar–early May and Oct–mid-Dec Wed–Sat 11am–4pm). It's worth pre-booking a tour (tel: 0492-76 94 00). Children will probably prefer the antics of the Pippi Longstocking impersonators at **Astrid Lindgrens Värld** (www.alv.se; May daily 10am–5pm, June–Aug daily

10am–6pm, Sept Fri–Sun 10am–5pm), with 100 larger-than-life settings from the stories.

THE KINGDOM OF CRYSTAL

Inland among the forests is the **Glasriket** ⑫ (Kingdom of Crystal; www.glasriket.se; most glassworks open summer Mon–Fri 10am–6pm, Sat–Sun 11am–4pm, winter shorter hours), a tremendously popular area of Småland between Nybro and Växjö containing several glassworks. Here you can buy crystal creations, watch hypnotic glass-blowing demonstrations, and even have a go yourself. Some companies will also arrange special Hyttsill Evenings (see page 103), which hark back to the days when herring was cooked in the heat from the furnaces.

King Gustav Vasa brought glass-blowers to Sweden in 1556, but it was another 200 years before the first glassworks, Kosta, was founded in Småland, fuelled by the province's abundance of wood. The company still exists today, but has merged with Orrefors and Åfors to create one mighty glassworks: its wares are marketed under the brand names 'Kosta Boda' and 'Orrefors'.

ASTRID LINDGREN AND PIPPI LONGSTOCKING

Astrid Lindgren (1907–2002), author of Pippi Långstrump (Longstocking), was born in Vimmerby in northeast Småland, which has now become a place of pilgrimage for both children and parents. Lindgren's most famous creation, the red-haired, anarchic Pippi Longstocking, was invented to entertain her young daughter when she was ill. Once published, these enchanting tales quickly became favourites in more than 60 languages. Lindgren wrote some 75 books in total, but no character has ever beaten Pippi for popularity.

In **Växjö**, 109km (68 miles) west of Kalmar, there is a **Glasmuseet** (Glass Museum; www.kulturparkensmaland. se; June–Aug daily 10am–5pm, Sept–May Tue–Fri 10am–5pm, Sat–Sun 11am–4pm) and the **House of Emigrants**, an interesting museum where you can learn why large numbers of Swedes emigrated to the USA.

The medieval wall at Visby

Northwest of Växjö, close to the border with Halland near **Anderstorp**, is Småland's version of the Wild West, a ranch-style theme park called **High Chaparral** (www.highchaparral. se; June–mid-Aug daily10am–6pm, 2nd half of Aug Fri–Sun 10am–6pm) with cowboy-inspired shows, rides and activities.

The northernmost tip of this large province's most fertile area stretches to the southern end of Lake Vättern (see page 61).

THE ISLANDS

The two southeastern Baltic islands, **Öland** and **Gotland**, are very different in style and character both from the mainland and each other. Öland is long and narrow, connected to Kalmar on the mainland by one of Europe's longest **bridges**, with 6km (almost 4 miles) of slender arches. Gotland is the Baltic's largest island at 120km (90 miles) long and 40km (30 miles) wide, and has the most hours of sunshine in Sweden.

ÖLAND

The remarkable bridge to Öland transports you into a different, outdoorsy world. The southern part of the island is dominated by the huge limestone plateau **Stora Alvaret**, a botanist's dream with wild flowers galore, including 40 species of orchid: its rich biodiversity has earned it Unesco World Heritage status.

The plateau was inhabited in prehistoric times, and ancient burial grounds are scattered across it. **Eketorp** (www.eketorp. se; mid-June–mid-Aug daily 10.30am to 5pm, second half of Aug Wed–Sun 10.30am–6pm), one of several later Iron Age ring forts, was rebuilt in the Middle Ages: in summer it hums with medieval re-enactors and craftspeople.

Right at the southern tip of the island, you'll find Sweden's tallest lighthouse, **Långe Jan**, and **Ottenby bird station**, one of Sweden's best birdwatching sites. Over 370 species have been recorded here, and migrants, such as honey buzzards, can sweep past in huge numbers.

Öland Zoo and Amusement Park (www.olandsdjurpark. com), lying just below the bridge, has long been patronised by the royal family, who stay on Öland at Solliden, their summer home. Öland's 'capital', **Borgholm ⑬**, is north of the bridge, and boasts Scandinavia's largest **castle ruins** (www.borgholm sslott.se; Apr–Sept daily 10am–4pm, May–Aug 10am–6pm), which are worth taking your time over.

GOTLAND

Gotland's population of 57,000 is swelled by two million visitors every year, thanks to its fine beaches and vibrant café and bar scene. Dotted with ancient churches, rune stones and windmills, Gotland is a delight for history lovers. The flat landscape is perfect for cyclists, and many take to their tandems to appreciate the wild flowers that bloom all over the island.

Visby ⑭ was once an important trading centre during the Hanseatic period, the German legacy of which shows in the town's fairy-tale architecture, deemed worthy of Unesco World Heritage status. In total, 3km (2 miles) and 44 towers remain of the medieval walls. Within the old walls, much of the medieval city still stands: step-gabled houses with red pantile roofs, narrow streets, buildings like **Gamla Apotek** (the old pharmacy), and the three towers of **Domkyrkan Sankta Maria** (the cathedral).

Gotland still possesses 90 medieval churches, a tribute to the wealth of the farmers in the years before Visby gained the trade monopoly. Every year in August, **Medeltidsveckan** (Medieval Week; www.medeltidsveckan.se) turns back time to remember its golden era; Gotlanders don medieval costumes to revel as merchants, monks and high-born ladies and enjoy the markets, music and theatre.

Like Öland, Gotland offers many outdoor attractions. The largest forest, Lojstaskogen, still has a wild herd of an unusual breed of ponies with two toes, called *Russ* since they are believed to have come from Russia (*Ryssland* in Swedish). There are also two good islands for birdwatching just south of Visby.

Sea stack, Gotland

North of Visby, one of the island's best sights is found at **Lummelundagrottan** ⑮ (www.lummelundagrottan.se; guided tours May–Sept daily), where the magnificent limestone caves are lined with huge stalactites.

Fårö, the Sheep Island, north of Gotland, was home to renowned film director Ingmar Bergman. There are fantastic *Raukar* stone formations and beautiful sandy beaches here.

A view over Gothenburg harbour

GOTHENBURG AND THE WEST

GOTHENBURG

Gothenburg 16 (Göteborg) made its fortune from shipbuild-ing, and is still Scandinavia's busiest port. It's exciting to arrive by sea, standing on deck as the land creeps towards you. The ship heads through a maze of small islands and into the mouth of the Götaälv, past the ruins of Älvsborg Fortress, which once guarded this entrance, and the beau-tiful Vinga nature reserve. Ahead is the high curve of the Älvsborg Bridge.

Sailing past Lilla Bommen harbour, you can't miss **Skan-skaskrapan**, a 1980s red-and-white office block known colloquially as 'the Lipstick'. On its 22nd floor, the **Utkiken** ('lookout'; July daily 11am–4pm, rest of the year Mon–Fri 11am–3pm) provides spectacular views of the city and harbour. Opposite is the **Göteborgsoperan** (Opera House; http://sv.opera.se), the size of two city blocks. Many **day**

cruises leave from Lilla Bommen harbour, to the nearby **Älvsborg Fortress** or further afield into the beautiful **Gothenburg Archipelago Ⓐ**.

Leave plenty of time to explore **Maritiman Ⓑ** (www.mariti man.se; June–Aug daily 10am–6pm, May and Sept daily 11am– 5pm), a fabulous collection of 20 vintage ships moored along Packhuskajen.

Two kilometres (1.2 miles) further down the river, **Sjöfarts- museet Akvariet** (Maritime Museum and Aquarium; www. sjofartsmuseum.goteborg.se; Tue–Sun 10am–5pm, Wed until 8pm) explores the city's maritime history and shows off Sweden's marine life. In front of the museum, on the 44m- (142ft-) tall **Sjöfartstornet** tower, stands a tender statue of a sailor's wife gazing out to sea.

HISTORICAL SIGHTS

Gothenburg was founded in 1603 by Karl IX, next to what was then Sweden's only outlet to the western sea. The city hud- dled around Älvsborg Fortress, but this was captured by the Danes in 1612 during the Kalmar War. They ransomed it for one million Riksdalers, a sum that took more than six years to pay, by which time the town had almost crumbled away. It was refounded in 1619 by Karl IX's son, Gustav II Adolf, com- memorated by a statue in **Gustav Adolfs Torg**.

Gustav saw Gothenburg as Sweden's western trad- ing gateway; he enlisted Dutch builders, who designed a layout with a moat and canals. Two canals remain, giving Gothenburg its characteristic style, which is best appreci- ated by taking a **Paddan Boat Ⓒ** (literally, 'Toad Boat') from Kungsportsplatsen.

Periodic fires destroyed the oldest wooden buildings, and today Gothenburg is a jumble of dates and styles. The surviv- ing structures from those early days are all stone-built: part of

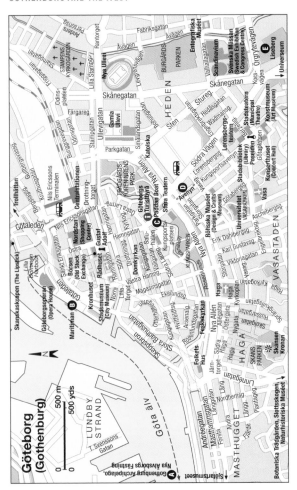

Göteborg (Gothenburg)

Fabriksgatan

Entoprafiska Museet

Scandinavium

Svenska Mässan (Swedish Exhibition & Congress Centre)

Örgrytevägen

Liseberg

Universeum

Skånegatan

HEDEN

Stureg

Stadsteatern (Municipal Theatre)

Konstmuseum (Art Museum)

Konserthuset (Concert Hall)

Stadsbibliotek (Library)

Lorensbergs-teatern

Södra Vägen

Nya Ullevi

STAMPENS KYRKOGÅRDEN

Lilla Stamp

Odins-platsen

Färgaregt

Gamla Ullevi

Parkgatan

Katolska

VASASTADEN

Vasa

Götaplatsen

Poseidon

Universitet

Erik Dahlbergsg.

Karl Gustavsg.

Viktoriagatan

Engelbrektsg.

Ascheberg

TRÄDGÅRDS-FÖRENINGENS PARK

Nya Allén

Göteborgs Turistbyrå

Stora Teatern

Paddan Boat

Rohsska Museet (Design & Crafts Museum)

Kungsportsavenyn

Avenyn

Centralstationen

Nils Ericssons Terminalen

Nordstan Shopping Centre

Gustaf Adolf

Rådhuset

Domkyrkan

Börsen (Old Stock Exchange)

Hamngatan

Kungsportsplatsen

KUNGSPARKEN

Rosenlund

Magasinsgatan

Ekelundsg.

Feskekyrkan

Haga

Nya Allén

Kronhuset

Stadsmuseum (City Museum)

Maritiman

Skanskaskrapen (The Lipstick)

Göteborgsoperan (Opera House)

Götaleden

Nils Ericssonsg

Skeppsbron

Stora Badhusgatan

Folkets Hus

Arsenalg.

SKANS PARKEN

Skansen Kronan

HAGA

Linnégatan

Nordhemsg.

MASTHUGGET

Masthamnsgatan

Andréegatan

Plantageg.

LUNDBY STRAND

T. Svenssons Gatan

Göta älv

N

0   500 m
0   500 yds

Gothenburg Archipelago, Nya Älvsborgs Fästning

Sjöfartsmuseet

Botaniska Trädgården, Slottsskogen, Naturhistoriska Museet

the old wall, **Bastion Carolus Rex** at Kungsgatan; the **Skansen Lejonet** and **Skansen Kronan** forts; and Gothenburg's oldest building, the Dutch-style **Kronhuset** (1643), once the city armoury. It briefly became the House of Parliament in 1660, when Karl X Gustav died suddenly in the city and his four-year-old son came to the throne. Next to Kronhuset are the **Kronhusbodarna** (www.kronhusbodarna.com), two rows of 18th-century artillery stores and blacksmiths' forges. Today they house a few modern crafts workshops and a chocolatier.

On the west side of Gustav Adolfs Torg is the **Rådhuset** (City Hall), built in 1672, and to the north, **Börsen**, the old Stock Exchange. The first of the big canals, **Stora Hamnkanalen**, runs past the southern edge of the square, with fine mercantile buildings along its banks. On the north (Norra Hamngatan) is **Ostindiska Huset**, the Swedish East India Company's premises, now home to the **Stadsmuseum** (City Museum; http://goteborgsstadsmuseum.se; Tue–Sun 10am–5pm, Wed until 8pm; everyone under 25 free), which documents Gothenburg's history and also contains Sweden's only Viking ship.

In contrast to all this history, northeast of Gustav Adolfs Torg is the **Nordstan** shopping centre (http://nordstan.se). An arcade covers the old central street, leading to Central Station and the bus terminus.

WALKING DOWN THE AVENUE

The city is compact, and easy to see on foot (or by tram or bus). Particularly popular with strollers is **Avenyn** ⓓ (Kungsportsavenyn), which is more like a French boulevard than a Swedish street. Lined with trees, shops and cafés spilling onto the wide pavements, it is always full of people – musicians, vendors or locals just out for a wander and a chat. It starts at busy **Kungsportsplatsen**, where a statue of Karl IX stands before the main **tourist office**.

A Paddan Boat passes the Stora Teatern

Crossing over **Rosenlundskanalen** (the Paddan Boat terminus), you'll see the splendid 19th-century theatre **Stora Teatern** on the right. Behind it, **Kungsparken** lies along the canal. Opposite the theatre, Trädgårdsföreningen is a popular park (see page 59). A little farther on, to the right off Avenyn, is the **Röhsska Museet** (www.designmuseum.se; Tue noon–8pm, Wed–Fri noon–5pm, Sat–Sun 11am–5pm), with a notable exhibition of modern design.

At the south end of Avenyn is **Götaplatsen**, guarded by Carl Milles' fountain statue of **Poseidon**, which shocked citizens at its 1931 unveiling (Too big! Too naked! Where's his beard?). Gothenburg's main cultural institutions flank the square: **Stadsteatern** (City Theatre; most events are in Swedish); Konstmuseet (Art Museum); **Konserthuset** (Concert Hall, and home to the city's Symphony Orchestra); the **Stadsbibliotek** (City Library); and **Lorensbergsteatern**.

The **Konstmuseum** (www.konstmuseum.goteborg.se; Tue and Thu 11am–6pm, Wed 11am–8pm, Fri–Sun 11am–5pm) houses a wonderful collection of Scandinavian paintings, many from the Nordic Light period at the turn of the 20th century, when young artists met at Skagen in north Denmark. This era is portrayed in the painting *Hip, Hip, Hurra!*, P.S. Krøyer's depiction of the artists toasting one another.

AMUSEMENT PARKS AND GARDENS

Gothenburg's major attraction is **Liseberg** ❸ (www.liseberg.se; daily mid-May–mid-Aug – see website for times), Sweden's biggest amusement park, located beyond Götaplatsen. Attractions include the 145km/h (90mph) wooden roller-coaster, Balder; and AtmosFear, one of Europe's tallest free-fall attraction. Kids will also love the nearby **Universeum** (www.universeum.se; daily 10am–6pm, longer hours in summer), a state-of-the-art nature centre with everything from rainforest butterflies to sharks.

Gothenburg prides itself on its parks. The most unexpected is **Trädgårdsföreningen** (Trägår'n; http://tradgardsforeningen.se; park daily 7am–6pm, May–Sept until 8pm), at the heart of the city on the banks of Rosenlundskanalen. Founded in 1842, it has rose gardens, beautiful statues and an elegant glass palm house.

Gothenburg's largest park is 137-hectare (340-acre) **Slottsskogen** (Castle Wood), reached via Linnégatan, with its own penguin pool. Here too is the **Naturhistoriska Museet** (www.gnm.se; Tue–Sun 11am–5pm), Sweden's oldest **Deer Park** and a zoo.

To the southeast, across Dag Hammarskjöldsleden, is Gothenburg's **Botaniska Trädgården** (Botanic Garden; www.gotbot.se), with more than 4,000 species in its massive rock garden. On the way to Slottsskogen, stop at **Feskekörka** (www.feskekörka.se), a fine fish market housed in a church-like building on the north side of Rosenlundskanalen. It also has a good fish restaurant, **Restaurang Gabriel** (http://restauranggabriel.se). On the other side of the canal is the

Trädgårdsföreningen

former working-class district of **Haga**, with cobbled streets, 19th-century wooden houses, and little shops and cafés.

THE COAST

The coasts on either side of Gothenburg are ideal places for bathing and lazing. This whole region is popular with Swedes, who come to stay in their *stugor* (rustic summer retreats). Sweden's 'summer capital' **Marstrand**, a yachties' playground and holiday destination of the royal family, is dominated by the impressive Carlsten's Fortress.

Bohuslän to the north is an ancient province. Don't miss the Bronze Age rock carvings at the Unesco World Heritage Site **Tanum** ⓱. The **Vitlycke Hällristningsmuseum** (Rock Carvings Museum; www.vitlyckemuseum.se; Apr Sat–Sun 11am–4pm, May–Aug daily 10am–6pm, Sept daily 10am–4pm, Oct Tue–Sun 11am–4pm) organises a number of guided tours, including night-time tours of the unearthly petroglyphs – bring your own torch. Nearby, picture-perfect **Fjällbacka** is the birthplace of thriller-writer Camilla Läckberg, and forms the backdrop to some of her murders. North of Strömstad, the Swedish–Norwegian frontier is marked by a fjord and a high bridge.

The small, thinly populated province of Dalsland, north of Bohuslän, has many lakes, and it is a paradise for boat-lovers. **Bengtsfors** and **Dals-Ed**, two villages joined by an isthmus with a lake on either side, enjoy some of the nation's most beautiful views. The **Dalsland Canal** weaves its way through a gentle landscape and over the awesome **Håverud Aqueduct** on its journey south to Lake Vänern.

Halland, to the south of Gothenburg, is a family favourite for its seaside towns, such as **Varberg**, **Kungsbacka**, **Laholm**, **Halmstad** and **Falkenberg**. (Varberg has ferries to Grenå in Denmark.) In 2017, Halmstad will be one of the Scandinavian ports welcoming the Tall Ships' Races, a spectacular event that showcases large sailing ships. East of Kungsbacka, 26km (18 miles) south of Gothenburg, stands **Fjärås Bräcka** – a great ridge, formed by ancient glaciers, scattered with Bronze and Iron Age grave fields.

THE LAKES

Sweden's great lakes lie to the northeast of Gothenburg. At 5,650 sq km (2,180 sq miles), **Lake Vänern** is the largest freshwater lake in Western Europe, while **Lake Vättern**, at 2,000 sq km (750 sq miles), is the second-largest in Sweden. East of Vänern is the **Göta Kanal** ⓲ (see box page 62), which links with Lake Vättern en route to Stockholm.

Archipelago boats

Several companies offer cruises around the archipelago: check out www.stromma.se, www.walona.se and www.steamboat.se. Local inter-island boats run to the southern archipelago from Saltholmen harbour (your tram ticket from Gothenburg centre is also valid on the boats).

In summer, these huge lakes are dotted with boats and swimmers, and the shores with fishermen hooking salmon. Vänern feels like a sea in the middle of Sweden, with Dalsland to the west and **Värmland** and **Västergötland** to the north and east. Värmland, along the Norwegian border, is wild and forested.

One of Sweden's most beautiful rivers, Klarälven, flowing south to join Vänern at Karlstad, was once used to float logs to the paper mills, a practice that continued right up to 1991. Today **rafting holidays** (www.sverigeflotten.com) are popular. **Karlstad**, 400 years old, was once a trading post and a resting place on the pilgrim route, which followed the Klarälven to the grave of St Olav the Holy at Trondheim in Norway.

Two other lakeside towns are **Mariestad** to the east, with the towering spire of its 17th-century church, and, in the south, **Lidköping**, a former porcelain town and home to the **Rörstrand Museum** (www.rorstrand-museum.se; Mon–Sat 10am–5pm, Sun noon–5pm; free), containing some unique pieces. Between

THE GÖTA CANAL

The Göta Canal (Kanal in Swedish), an astonishing feat of 18th-century engineering, threads through 190km (118 miles) of beautiful countryside from Gothenburg to Stockholm. The classic way to navigate this popular waterway is on a four-day cruise aboard a vintage vessel, run by the Göta Canal Steamship Company (www.stromma.se). En route, the canal winds through small towns, past peaceful shores where osprey and heron breed, and across the sea-like Great Lakes Vättern and Vänern.

If you prefer to take a more hands-on approach, you could charter your own motorboat or hire a canoe (several companies offer a pick-up service so you don't have to retrace your journey). For landlubbers, the track alongside the Göta Canal is Sweden's most popular cycling path. For full details, see www.gotakanal.se.

the two towns is **Kinnekulle**, a beautiful 350m (1,150ft) hill called the 'flowering mountain'.

North of Lidköping on the **Kållandsö Peninsula** is one of Sweden's finest castles, the restored 17th-century **Läckö Slott** ⑲ (www.lacko slott.se; mid-June–Aug daily 10am–6pm, May–mid-June and Sept daily 10am–3pm by

Ship on the Göta Kanal

on-the-hour guided tours only; charge), which holds popular operatic evenings. Great houses dot the areas close to the lakes; Värmland has two in particular. **Rottneros Manor**, on Lake Fryken, is considered by many to be the most beautiful in Sweden, while **Mårbacka** (www.marbacka.com; June and Aug daily 11am–4pm, July 10am–5pm,May and Sept Sat–Sun 11am–2pm, Oct–Apr guided tours only Sat 2pm), on the other side of the lake, was the home of Swedish writer Selma Lagerlöf (1858–1940), in 1909 the first woman to receive a Nobel prize.

On the west shore of Lake Vättern, **Karlsborgs Fästning** (www. karlsborgsfastning.se) is a staggering 19th-century bastion, built to hide the royal family and the nation's gold in the event of Russian takeover. The **fortress museum** (www.fastningsmuseet. se; mid-May–Aug daily 10am–4pm/5pm/6pm, Oct–mid-May Mon–Fri 10am–3pm) explores its history. **Jönköping**, at the lake's southernmost point, is the capital of north Småland. The safety match was invented here: the old factory is now the world's only match museum, **Tändsticksmuseet** (www.matchmuseum. se; June–Aug Mon–Fri 10am–5pm, Sat–Sun 10am–3pm, Sept–May Tue–Sun11am–3pm; Nov–Feb free). Fairy-tale illustrator John Bauer was born in Jönköping: the town museum (www.

jkpglm.se; Tue–Fri noon–7pm, Wed until 9pm, Sat–Sun 11am–5pm; free) contains his exquisite drawings, heavily influenced by Småland's forests. To the east is **Huskvarna**, where weapons were made 300 years ago, before the Husqvarna company diversified into sewing machines and chainsaws: the **Husqvarna Fabriksmuseum** (www.husqvarnamuseum.se; May–Sept Mon–Fri 10am–5pm, Sat–Sun noon–4pm, Oct–Apr Mon–Fri 10am–3pm, Sat–Sun noon–4pm) tells all.

North from Jönköping on the lovely lakeside road is the idyllic little town of **Gränna** ⑳. This was the birthplace of aviator S.A. Andrée, who in 1897 tried unsuccessfully to cross the North Pole in a hot-air balloon. Each year Gränna celebrates the flight with balloon events; there are many related exhibits in the **Andrée Museet** (www.grennamuseum.se; June–Aug daily 10am–6pm, Sept–May 10am–4pm). While here, try the local specialities: luscious pears and *polkagrisar*, a red-and-white peppermint rock you can watch being made in one of the *polkagrisar* bakeries.

From Gränna it's just a short boat trip to the narrow isle of **Visingsö**. Here, horse-drawn carriages take visitors to the ruins of the 17th-century **Visingsborgs Slott**, which held prisoners during Karl XII's wars with Russia.

Farther north and, thanks to the Holy Birgitta, on a grander scale, is **Vadstena**, with its beautiful 14th-century church. Born in 1303, Birgitta gave up her temporal life at the age of 40 after having six children. She moved to Rome and founded the St Birgittine Order. After her death, her body was brought back to Vadstena. Over a century later, Gustav Vasa, architect of the Swedish Reformation, built a great fortress castle nearby. Both church and castle are still standing.

THE CENTRAL HEARTLANDS

Seven provinces link the south of Sweden to its vast northern stretches. They are the coastal provinces of Gästrikland,

Hälsingland, Medelpad and Ångermanland, and the inland provinces of Dalarna, Härjedalen and Jämtland – the last two both great sweeps of forest, river and rising mountains. Even though they are on the eastern side of the country, Medelpad and Ångermanland form the county known, oddly enough, as Västernorrland – or West Norrland.

Vadstena Castle

DALARNA

Dalarna is the heart of all things Swedish, where the old traditions and costumes are as natural a part of feast days as they were 100 years ago. Its tiny hamlets are scattered around the sparkling shores of **Lake Siljan ㉑**, gouged out 350 million years ago by a falling meteorite.

Nowhere is the feast of **Midsommar** (Midsummer) celebrated more enthusiastically than in these lakeside communities, where the wooden houses are painted a special dark red with white trim. Dancers kick their heels around Sweden's national maypole just outside **Leksand**, boosting their energy with traditional dishes. In June, local people in costume row long 'church-boats' to **Rättvik Kyrka** at the southeastern end of the lake, recreating the times when this was the easiest way to journey in from outlying farms.

Perched above Siljan and affording lovely views, **Tällberg** is one of the most popular holiday spots. **Nusnäs** is the main source of the *Dalahäst* (Dala horse), the carved, brightly painted wooden statuettes. During the summer you can watch the carving and painting in the small factory, **Nils Olsson Hemslöjd** (www.nohemslojd.se; free).

At **Mora**, **Zorngården** (part of the **Zorn Museum**; www.zorn.se; mid-May–mid-Sept Mon–Sat 9am–5pm, Sun 10.45am–5pm, mid-Sept–mid-Nov daily 11.45am–5pm, mid-Nov–mid-May 11.45am–4pm) was the home of **Anders Zorn** (1860–1920), a painter whose lavish works were part of the National Romantic movement of the time. His studio is as he left it. Mora is also the finishing line for the world's biggest ski race, the gruelling 90km (56-mile) **Vasaloppet** (www.vasaloppet.se), rooted in a powerful Swedish legend (see box page 68) and celebrated in the town's dedicated museum. Nearby **Sälen** is Scandinavia's largest ski resort, with 116 runs among the surrounding mountains.

Bears at the **Orsa Grönklitt Bear Park** ㉒ (www.orsabjornpark.se; mid-June–mid-Aug 10am–6pm, mid-Aug–mid-June 10am–3pm), a little farther north, roam the natural forest of their large enclosures. Visitors walk to special viewing platforms for a superb view of the bears and the surrounding countryside. The park is also home to wolves and lynx.

There are fine views from the hill **Gesundaberget**, 514m (1,650ft) high, home to a southerly **Santaworld** (Tomteland; www.santaworld.se), which offers animals, toy workshops and a resident Santa. For more information on the area, see www.siljan.se.

Unusual spring

If you are visiting Rättvik in winter, check out the unusual spring by the Draggån River (6km/4 miles north of Rättvik, just beyond the racetracks). In 1869 a prospector drilled for oil here, but found highly pressurised water instead. Since then the water has gushed out year-round, and during winter forms stunning natural ice formations.

Lake Siljan in Dalarna

FALUN

Falun and its surroundings are a paradise for industrial archaeologists, thanks to their mineral-rich earth and a long mining history, and the whole area forms a Unesco World Heritage Site. Copper-mining in Falun dates back to at least the 8th century. By the 17th century, the town produced 70 percent of the world's copper.

The most dramatic symbol of all this activity is the Great Pit at **Falu Gruva** ㉓ (Falun Mine; www.falugruva.se; daily tours year-round, Apr–Sept daily, Oct–Mar Tue–Sun), created by a vast pit collapse in 1687. Take the one-hour underground tour to discover more about the early miners who worked in such dangerous conditions. The 800-year-old mine closed down in 1992, but 'Falun Red', the colour used to paint Sweden's distinctive red wooden houses, is still made here from iron-based pigments.

In the nearby village of Sundborn is **Carl Larsson-Gården** ㉔ (www.clg.se; 45-minute tours May–Sept daily 10am–5pm,

Oct–Apr Mon–Fri 11am and Sat–Sun 1pm), the idyllic home of painter Carl Larsson (1853–1919) and his family. It's an inspirational place, filled with colour and light, and still serves as a template for Swedish interior design.

GÄSTRIKLAND AND HÄLSINGLAND

Life in tiny Gästrikland centres on its main town, **Gävle**. Here is a **Railway Museum** (www.trafikverket.se/Museer/Sveriges-Jarnvagsmuseum-Gavle; Tue–Sun 10am–4pm), including an 1874 coach of the veteran traveller *King Oscar II*. Some 10km (6 miles) south of Gävle is **Furuviksparken** (www.furuvik.se; daily in summer), a theme park and zoo, on a lovely stretch of waterfront with amazing gardens.

THE VASALOPPET

Every March in Dalarna, 15,000 competitors take to their skis for one of the world's most demanding endurance races. The 90km (56-mile) Vasaloppet, which begins in Sälen and ends in Mora, was first held in 1922 and today has grown into the country's most popular sporting event. A Vasaloppet victory is regarded just as highly as an Olympic podium place.

Part of the Vasaloppet's powerful grip on the Swedish psyche lies in its legendary roots. After the Stockholm Bloodbath of 1520, when the Danish King Christian II executed 82 Stockholm citizens, nobleman Gustav Vasa headed for Mora in a last-ditch attempt to raise a rebel army against the Danes. The locals were lukewarm, and Gustav cut his losses, strapped on his skis and fled for the Norwegian border. In the meantime, the community had a change of heart, and sent their two fastest skiers to intercept Gustav. They succeeded: Gustav returned to Mora, raised his army, defeated the Danish king, and the Swedish nation was born. Today's race is skied in memory of that epic winter chase.

The main road, the E4, sets out across Sweden's immense distances, passing Söderhamn and Hudiksvall (Hälsingland's two principal coastal towns) before reaching the dramatic High Coast. Söderhamn goes back to the 17th century, when it was built as an army town (the armoury is now a museum).

The Great Pit at Falun Mine

The pace of life slows in the coast's numerous fishing villages, where Baltic herring comes into its own – served with dill, or sometimes smoked golden brown and called *böckling*. Herring from **Bönan**, not far north of Gävle, is particularly famous.

The old, prosperous ironmasters of this area left their legacy in many places, including the **Galtström Bruk** (Galtström Ironworks; www.galtstromsbruk.se; May–Aug daily), in the Medelpad region. Built in 1673 and closed in 1917, the whole site, from blast furnace and foundry to elegant manor house and workers' dwellings, is in excellent condition. There is also a delightful café and restaurant.

In the same valley, on the E14 from Sundsvall and Ånge, **Flataklocken** rises to 465m (1,500ft). If you took a rigid map of Sweden and balanced it on a pin, the 'balancing point' would be under Flataklocken. There's a road to the top, and an observation tower with far-reaching panoramas.

Hälsingland has a rich folk-music history – contact the tourist office to find out more about local 'fiddlers' meets' (*spelmansstämma*). The area may revel in all things traditional, but even tradition can be created afresh. Inaugurated in 2011, **Musik vid Dellen** is a two-week celebration of music and dance, taking

A summer farm in Dalarna

place in venues (farms, mills, churches and mountain pastures) across the district (www.visitgladahudik.se).

GULF OF BOTHNIA AND THE HIGH COAST

Sundsvall, on the Gulf of Bothnia, is largely stone, risen from the ashes of the disastrous Great Fire of 1888. At that time, it was the centre of the sawmill industry, and was rebuilt in grand architectural style by its wealthy timber barons.

Several northern towns on the Gulf of Bothnia suffered in Swedish–Russian conflicts. After **Härnösand** was raided in 1721, few of the early buildings were left, apart from the wooden houses in **Östanbäcken**. The best view of the town and harbour is from **Murberget** (www.murberget.se; Tue–Sun 11am–4pm; free), an open-air museum second only to Stockholm's magnificent Skansen.

The sweeping suspension bridge **Högakustenbron**, around 14km (8.5 miles) north of Härnosand, is the start of the beautiful **Höga Kusten** ㉕ (High Coast; www.hogakusten.com; see box page 72). Here, Sweden's highest cliffs stretch alongside a glittering sea, 80km (48 miles) north to Örnsköldsvik, with the **Nordingrå peninsula** as their centre. The High Coast is hard to see from the E4 and has remained little known. The simplest detour is to turn right off the road at Gallsäter into a world of cliffs, inlets, islands, tiny villages, wonderful places to swim and restaurants offering a taste of *husman-skost* (home cooking).

At the northern end of the High Coast, **Varvsberget** rises out of the town of Örnsköldsvik (also known as Övik). The mountain affords a good view over the Gulf of Bothnia and nearby islands like Ulvön and Trysunda, still home to genuine fishermen-farmers. Their villages have a number of lovely old fishing chapels to visit, and you can still purchase salmon from a fridge on the jetty, leaving payment in the 'honesty box'.

HÄRJEDALEN AND JÄMTLAND

Where the great rivers rise in the mountains of Härjedalen and Jämtland, close to the Norwegian border, you will come across some magnificent waterfalls. **Tännforsen** ㉖, west of Östersund, is the most famous in Sweden, with a drop of 30m (100ft) in a massive white wall which becomes the river Indalsälven.

Farther north, **Hällingsåfallet** has, over thousands of years, bitten into the surrounding rock face to form Europe's largest filled canyon. There is the thrill of white-water rafting on many of these rivers, as well as canoeing and some superb fishing.

The slopes of Härjedalen and Jämtland offer facilities for skiing, walking and climbing, as well as mountain-biking and pony-trekking. The forests are carpeted with delicate flowers and wild berries such as raspberries, blueberries and *hjortron* (cloudberries) – all favourites in the Swedish pastime of **berry-picking**.

Härjedalen is the highest province in Sweden, with the highest village, **Tännäs**, and the highest A-road (84), which runs over the **Flatruet Plateau**. From here you can get a good view of Sweden's most southerly glacier on **Helagsfjället**, just east of the Norwegian border. At 1,796m (6,000ft), this is Sweden's highest peak south of the Arctic Circle.

The way into these wild spots is from the south on the E45 or east–west from Hudiksvall on Highway 84, following the course of the River Ljusnan. The two highways intersect at **Sveg**, Härjedalen's biggest town (with 2,500 inhabitants). Sveg's open-air museum, **Gammelgården** (May–Sept daily 11am–5pm), has 20 old buildings. The **King's Stone**, erected in 1909, marks the arrival of the railway in the town, while the railway bridge over the quiet waters of the Ljusnan is a masterpiece of engineering. A relaxing way to travel into Härjedalen and Jämtland is by rail, with good links from the south. For railway connoisseurs, the scenic *Inlandsbanan* line (see page 132) runs through the two provinces, stopping at Sveg, Östersund and several smaller stations. Sveg is also the town where Swedish crime-fiction writer Henning Mankell

EXPLORING THE HIGH COAST

The scenic Höga Kusten area has been designated a Unesco World Heritage Site due to its unique geology. When the ice melted at the end of the last Ice Age, the land here was freed from the heavy glaciers that once weighted it down. Like a coiled spring being released, the Höga Kusten is rising at a rate of 8mm per year – one of the fastest examples of glacio-isostatic uplift in the world.

The whole area is spectacularly beautiful: Sweden's highest cliffs tower over the boats and scattered red-granite islands of the Bothnian sea. It's best explored slowly, on foot, by bicycle, by boat. A great starting point is Skuleskogens National Park, which contains some of Sweden's best hiking trails, with magnificent views over untouched wilderness, cairns from the Bronze Age and lots of fresh blueberries to pick along the way. The Naturum Höga Kusten (Höga Kusten Visitor Centre; www.naturumhogakusten.se; Mar–mid-Apr daily 10am–5pm, May–mid-June and mid-Aug–Sept daily 10am–5pm, mid-June–mid-Aug 9am–7pm; free) contains a fascinating exhibition, as well as information on trails and cabins.

was brought up, and it boasts a Mankell Culture Centre.

Lake Storsjön ㉗ is to this area what Lake Siljan is to Dalarna. Sweden's fifth-largest lake lies in the centre of the two provinces, and contains the beautiful island of **Frösön**, named after the Norse god of fertility. **Frösö Kyrka**, built over an ancient sacrificial grove, is popular

The spectacular Tännforsen

for weddings. Every summer Frösön is the venue for performances of the well-known Viking story *Arnljot*, turned into an opera by local composer Wilhelm Peterson-Berger (1867–1942). Frösön also boasts **Frösö Zoo** (www.frosozoo.se; mid-June–mid-Aug daily 10am–4pm, July until 6pm), with more than 700 species. A trip to the top of **Frösö Tornet**, some 468m (1,560ft) high, will reward the climber with superb views.

The country's northernmost Viking rune stone is at the end of the footbridge linking Frösön to Jämtland's biggest town, **Östersund**. The main attraction here is **Jamtli Museet** (www.jamtli.com; mid-June–mid-Aug daily 11am–5pm, rest of the year Tue–Sun 11am–5pm), with some amazing 1,000-year-old tapestries, and a display of monster-catching gear. A creature like Scotland's 'Nessie' is said to lurk in the depths of Lake Storsjön – take a cruise in the coal-fired steamship, S/S *Östersund*, and see if you can spot it. In 2018, Jamtli Museet is to set to have a younger brother, a new branch of the Swedish National Museum that will be housed in a state-of-the-art building.

Farther north in **Åre** ㉘ (www.visitare.com) is one of the finest ski resorts in the country. The town lies on the slopes

Getting around on a reindeer sledge

of the 1,240m (4,500ft) **Åreskutan**, which towers above it. Skiers are taken by funicular railway from the town to half-way up the mountain, from where a cable car carries them to the summit.

For information on both regions, see www.jamtland.se.

NORRLAND AND THE ARCTIC

Norrland (the old Swedish name for 'the North') covers the provinces of Västerbotten, Norrbotten and Lappland. This huge, remote area stretches from the Gulf of Bothnia to the Norwegian border, and is punctuated by gleaming lakes, scented pine forests, and high mountain peaks – a heaven for outdoor types, with hiking, rafting and fishing opportunities, and all kinds of winter activities. One third of Norrland lies beyond the Arctic Circle, creating deep, dark winters and endless summer light. The largest towns lie along the coast at the mouths of Sweden's great rivers, a legacy of the 19th-century timber industry. Otherwise, long moorland miles separate its small communities.

Norrland is the heartland of the indigenous Sami people, who have inhabited the northern regions of Scandinavia and Russia for at least 2,500 years. They were originally called Lapps – hence Lappland – but Sami has become their preferred name. The enduring image of the Sami is as reindeer nomads, although only a small proportion of people make their living this way. In recent years, there has been a concerted effort to build up Sami cultural institutions and promote the Sami language, aided by the establishment of a Sami parliament in 1993.

UMEÅ AND THE NORRLAND RIVIERA

Driving north on the E4 will bring you to the rapidly expanding coastal town of **Umeå**, Norrland's largest. It is home to the region's only university: 39,000 of its 120,000 residents are students, giving it a young, lively atmosphere. The town has always been a strong cultural centre, with several popular music festivals, including a big Jazz Festival (www.umeajazzfestival.se) in October. Umeå was the European Capital of Culture 2014. The seven-storey **Bildmuseet** (www.bildmuseet.umu.se; Tue 11am–8pm, Wed–Sun 11am–6pm; free), opened in 2012 and is a super new exhibition space for the visual arts.

Västerbottens Museum (www.vbm.se; Mon–Fri 10am–5pm, Wed until 9pm, Sat–Sun 11am–5pm; free), houses skiing, fishing and maritime exhibitions, and includes an open-air section with a collection of historical buildings. **Umedalen sculpture park** (www.umedalenskulptur.se; free), 5km (3 miles) out of town, has some 40 works on display by international artists such as Louise Bourgeoise. The island of Holmön is Sweden's largest and sunniest offshore nature reserve, free of cars and with bicycles for hire.

As you head north, you'll see church villages from the days when a church served many far-flung communities. **Skellefteå**, though largely industrial, offers **Bonnstan Kyrkby**, a 400-year-old church town with various summer markets and events. The **town museum** (http://skellefteamuseum.se; Tue 10am–7pm, Wed–Sun 10am–4pm) has a separate boat museum with old vessels, which opens summer only.

From Skellefteå to Piteå, over the border in Norrbotten, the E4 clings to this beautiful coast, offering views of islands and headlands. The area's mild climate has earned it the nickname of the Norrland Riviera, and the warm Gulf waters certainly attract many visitors to sea resorts such as **Pite Havsbad** (www.pite-havsbad.se), with a long white sandy beach and a campsite.

As an alternative to the coastal route, turn northwest on road 374 to Älvsbyn and then continue to **Storforsen**, claimed to be Europe's highest falls, with a spectacular unbroken drop of 80m (250ft). Returning to Älvsbyn, take road 356 to **Boden** – Sweden's largest garrison town, a fortress built after the 1808–9

REINDEER HERDING

Of the 20,000 Sami in Sweden, only around 4,000 make a living from reindeer. Although life for many is still dictated by the reindeer, the Sami have adopted modern ways to ease their task: nowadays they herd with the aid of radios, dogs and motorcycles or snowscooters. They have kept the tradition of Sami communities, however, dividing themselves into Sami villages based on collective groups of reindeer owners who work together. The result may be that a community is not necessarily all in one place.

The Sami count, divide up their herds and mark the calves over two or three weeks during the summer, colourful occasions with lots of flying lassoes and careering reindeer. Most Sami people welcome visitors to watch – bear in mind, however, that this is not a spectacle, but the Sami way of earning a living.

war. (Parts of Norrbotten near this border are military areas subject to entry restrictions; details on road signs.) From Boden, Highway 97 runs alongside Luleälven to Luleå.

Sami knives

LULEÅ ARCHIPELAGO

The 300 islands forming the **Luleå Archipelago** are among the most beautiful in Sweden. **Luleå** itself is surrounded on all three sides by water. First founded by King Gustav II Adolf 10km (6 miles) farther up the estuary, the first harbour was too small; almost 30 years later, Luleå moved to the site it occupies today. The old town, **Gammelstad ㉙**, is listed as a Unesco World Heritage Site, as it is the biggest and best-preserved church town in existence, with 30 old farms and 450 cottages clustered round a 15th-century granite church.

Norrbottens Museum (www.norrbottensmuseum.se; Tue–Fri 10am–4pm, Sat–Sun 11am–4pm, mid-June–mid-Aug daily 11am–5pm) in Luleå houses a collection of Sami ethnography and stages temporary exhibitions. To the north is the Sami town of **Överkalix**, with its own distinctive dialect.

From Luleå, the E4 passes quite close to the northernmost waters of the Bothnian Gulf at **Kalix**, where the church has endured a turbulent history. Rebuilt after a fierce fire, it was ransacked in 1716 by Russians, who later used it as stables in the 1808–9 war.

THE INLAND WAY

There are two scenic routes for travelling in Sweden's northern interior, either the **Inlandsvägen** (road route, starting in

Gothenburg) or **Inlandsbanan** (rail, from Kristinehamn; see page 132). Detours are easier by car, but most Swedes use the train rather like a bus, leaving it for outdoor pursuits and rejoining it later.

The *Inlandsbanan* (http://inlandsbanan.se) offers a special guided railway tour from Östersund to Arvidsjaur, some 380km (228 miles) north, with a choice of stops and pursuits. At Gällivare the *Inlandsbanan* merges into the great east coast route from Stockholm (a long 16 hours away, best reached by sleeper). The route then continues to Kiruna and the border, 200km (130 miles) to the north.

Starting from Östersund by car (E45), the route to Dorotea lies through Jämtland and endless tracts of dense forest. Both road and rail run across dozens of small islands linked by bridges, and past lakes where you can see beavers and their handiwork.

Most small towns between **Dorotea** and **Arvidsjaur**, 250km (150 miles) north, have a church, a local museum and possibly a craft shop, giving a taste of the past. Dorotea's church has sculptures by the artist Carl Milles, and a life-size carving of the Last Supper by Björn Martinius.

The main town, **Vilhelmina**, had a large 18th-century church village; 24 of its houses survived a devastating fire, and have now been renovated for summer visitors. Sami crafts are on sale. The best time to visit is during the Kulturveckan celebrations in early July, which feature plenty of folk dancing and singing.

Heading north again, those with a car can divert west at Slagnäs (beyond Sorsele) onto a minor road that skirts the lovely waters of Storavan and Uddjaur, to the Sami town of **Arjeplog** ③, almost completely surrounded by water. The highlight here is the excellent **Silvermuseet** (www.silvermuseet.se; Mon–Fri 10am–5pm, Sat 10am–2pm), which shows off a huge collection of Sami artefacts gathered in the early 20th century by a young doctor, Einar Wallqvist, including a room full of Sami silver from the silver mines nearby. The 17th-century church is also worth a visit.

Arvidsjaur (www.polcirkeln. nu) still has the feel of a frontier town – not just because it is an army training-ground, but because it lies at the junction of five roads, and, 100 years ago, became a main trading post. In late August, the Sami people celebrate a festival (Storstämningshelgen) here, at the biggest Sami church village, **Lappstaden**.

Arvidsjaur is very much an outdoor place. **Piteälven**, to the north, is good for white-water rafting with the mag-

Traditional Sami dress, Norrland

nificent **Trollforsarna** (rapids); **Trollholmen**, an island that divides the river, is popular for walks, berry-picking and picnics. **Vittjåksfjällen** and **Prästberget** offer good skiing.

NORTH OF THE ARCTIC CIRCLE

Just before road and railway reach **Jokkmokk** ㉛ (160km/110 miles across marshland and forest to the north), you arrive at the Arctic Circle. Jokkmokk is in Sami territory; their great annual event, the **Jokkmokk Market** (www.jokkmokks marknad.se), first held here in 1605, takes place every year in the traditional spot at the beginning of February. Sami travel from Russia, Finland and Norway to meet and exchange news at the three-day event, donning their bright traditional dress and celebrating their culture. Visitors flock in to savour the

Sami atmosphere and buy typical Sami handiwork, but you have to book a year ahead to be sure of a bed.

The town's museum, **Ájtte** (www.ajtte.com; mid-June–mid-Aug daily 9am–6pm, mid-May–mid-June and mid-Aug–mid-Sept Tue–Fri 10am–4pm, Sat–Sun noon–4pm, mid-Sept–mid-May Tue–Fri 10am–4pm, Sat noon–4pm), covers the culture and myths of the Sami, as well as the hard world of the 18th- and 19th-century Swedish settlers. *Ájtte* is the Sami word for a store-house, and this is indeed a fine store of artefacts, historical tableaux and exhibitions, with a fascinating story to tell.

Southwest of Jokkmokk on Highway 97, the town of **Vuollerim** has the fascinating museum **Vuollerim 6000 År** (www.vuollerim6000.se; July–Aug Mon–Fri 10am–4pm, Sat–Sun 11am–4pm), built around the excavation of a 6,000-year-old hunting settlement and displaying well-preserved Stone Age tools and utensils.

Jokkmokk Kommun (district), the second largest in Sweden (roughly the size of Wales or Massachusetts), contains several vast national parks (of which **Muddus** is the closest to Jokkmokk town). It also boasts the country's wildest road, **Sjöfallsleden**, which branches northwest just after Porjus and passes through awe-inspiring scenery.

The road ends 170km (120 miles) farther on at **Ritsemjåkka**, high in the mountains, from where it is only another 18km (11 miles) on foot to the Norwegian Sea (Atlantic).

From **Saltuluokta**, halfway along the route, a boat also follows Sjöfallsleden. All around is the magical wilderness of the **Sarek**, **Padjelanta** and **Stora Sjöfallet National Parks** (see page 88).

Rail travellers to **Gällivare** will arrive at its very attractive 19th-century station. Gällivare's prosperity is built on mining. In nearby Malmberget, the huge pit **Gropen** splits the town in two, like a scene from Dante's *Inferno*. Two mining companies claw iron ore, copper, silver and gold from the region's ground: Gällivare tourist office (tel: 0970 166 60; www.gellivarelapland.se) can arrange mine tours in summer, while the **Gruvmuseet** (mining museum) illustrates 250 years of local mining history. The 823m (2,700ft) summit of Gällivare's **Dundret** gives a view of just under 10 percent of the whole of Sweden. The area is a great place for riding, walking, golf, rafting and skiing.

From Gällivare to Kiruna, rail and road part company, the latter merging into the E10 to Kiruna via **Svappavaara**. Here, the E45 comes into view again and heads northeast to **Karesuando**, which has Sweden's most northerly church, on the Finnish border.

KIRUNA AND BEYOND

Road and rail meet again at Kiruna. Until 1984, the road stopped here; the only way to Riksgränsen on the border with Norway was by rail. The road heads north along **Lake Torneträsk 32**, passing through some of the most remote and beautiful scenery in the world. You can experience round-the-clock sunlight from mid-June to early July.

Midnight sun

Kiruna is a mining town of 23,000 people with a lake at its centre, set between two mountains packed with ore. You can take a dramatic **underground tour** (by bus) of the mine, which has 400km (250 miles) of underground

The Northern Lights

roadways; the machines resemble prehistoric monsters. Book via the tourist office (www.kirunalapland.se; tel: 0980-188 80).

Incredibly, due to mining-related subsidence, over the next 20 years or so the whole town will be gradually moved to a new site, 3km (2 miles) east of today's city centre. Historical buildings will be physically relocated, while ordinary houses are to be built from scratch at the town's new location. The first buildings in the new centre should be completed in 2019.

About 21km (15 miles) east of Kiruna, **Jukkasjärvi** ㉝, on the Torneälven, is another world, with white-water rafting in the summer and impressive winter sports once the cold sets in. In Sami, *Jukkasjärvi* means meeting place, which it was for travellers of old on arduous treks through the great wilderness. Here is Lappland's oldest surviving wooden church, built in 1609, with a famous, brilliantly coloured altarpiece by Swedish artist Bror Hjort.

Jukkasjärvi is also home to Sweden's foremost hotel destination, the original **Ice Hotel** (www.icehotel.se). Each year the 'cold' part of the hotel is built from pure, clear ice from the River Torne, and filled with stunning ice sculptures created by international artists. A reindeer skin-covered bed in one of the -5 °C rooms comes with a premium price tag; but during the day, there are tours of the hotel so that everyone can admire its unique artwork. In the area, Arctic experiences await the adventurous, including snowmobiling, dog-sledding, and a naked dip into the frozen river.

At 2,111m (6,926ft), **Kebnekaise** ❸❹, west of Kiruna, is Sweden's highest mountain; it challenges even experienced walkers. It can form the climax of a hike along **Kungsleden**, a fine route that runs 86km (60 miles) from Abisko farther north, with overnight stops in mountain huts. This far to the north, from late May to late July, the sun never sets.

Whether by road or rail, the route to **Abisko Turiststation** (Abisko Mountain Station) is beautiful, offering views over the lovely waters of Torneträsk, and cutting through wilderness country with mountain peaks rising on both sides. The most noticeable heights are the twin summits that flank the deep semi-circle of **Lapporten**, the gateway to this last frontier.

Abisko has all the facilities you need to enjoy walking, mountain-biking and skiing, from accommodation to sports equipment hire to guided botany and ornithology tours. The national park visitor centre, **Naturum Abisko** (mid-Feb–Apr daily 2–6pm, mid-June–mid-Aug daily 9am–6pm, mid-Aug–Sept Tue–Sat 9am–6pm), has an informative exhibition on the **Abisko** and **Vadvetjåkka National Parks**.

Björkliden, approximately 7km (5 miles) to the north, has the highest-altitude mountain station in Sweden. At 1,228m (4,000ft), **Låktatjåkko** attracts skiers to its 15km (10 miles) of snow trails. In summer, it's covered in unique plants and there's access to the caves.

Northern Lights

If you are lucky during your time in the far north of Sweden, you may see the Northern Lights *(aurora borealis)*. This beautiful phenomenon often appears as a green mist whirling across the sky, or as a faint red tint like a strange sunset. This natural light show occurs mostly between September and October and March and April.

WHAT TO DO

Sweden is a natural playground, offering plentiful outdoor activities, from berry-picking to shooting rapids on a raft. Its well-rounded citizens are also blessed with an internationally renowned cultural scene: opera, theatre, art galleries and concerts all vie for your attention. At street level, Sweden is a shoppers' paradise, with everything from exclusive boutiques selling distinctive Scandinavian design to larger high-street stores catering to the stylish masses.

SPORTS

Swedes are true outdoor people: you'll find them everywhere, rowing, riding, cycling, hiking, swimming, playing football, ice hockey and bandy (similar to ice hockey), and teaching even the tiniest of their tots to ski. Orienteering is one of Sweden's most popular sports: around 100,000 people participate. At the end of May/early June Stockholm hosts one of Europe's biggest marathons.

SPECTATOR SPORTS

People flock to watch local and international sports at various stadiums and arenas. IFK-Göteborg, based at Gothenburg's Gamla Ullevi ground, and Malmö FF are the country's most successful football (soccer) teams. The Swedish ice-hockey team Tre Kronor plays at the Ericsson Globe (www.globearenas. se) in Stockholm, while the city's brand-new Friends Arena (https://friendsarena.se) hosts the finals of another fast-and-furious ice-based game, bandy. Tennis is another favourite: the Swedish Open is held at Båstad, on Skåne's southwest coast, in mid-July and the Stockholm Open in October. Major handball tournaments are held in Stockholm.

Canoeing around Stockholm's Gamla Stan

Åre is one of Sweden's most popular ski resorts

There are around 25 horse-racing and trotting tracks in Sweden, including Täby and Solvalla (Bromma) in Stockholm, Åby in Gothenburg, and Jägersro in Malmö. The Swedish Derby is held at Jägersro in September; and Gothenburg's International Horse Show takes place at the Scandinavium arena in February.

PARTICIPATORY SPORTS
Cycling. There are some pleasant bike trails in Sweden. Gotland is a cyclists' favourite, as is the scenic towpath alongside the Göta Canal. For the ambitious, Sverigeleden is a 9,500km (5,900 mile) network of cycle tracks, with the main section stretching from Helsingborg to Karesuando on the Finnish border.

Fishing. Vast stretches of pure water make for fine fishing in lake, river or sea. Superb salmon can be caught in lakes Vänern and Vättern, and even in central Stockholm. Freshwater fishing usually requires a permit, but sea fishing is free. Contact the Swedish Angling Federation (www.sport fiskarna.se) for further information, see www.swedenfishing. com, or order Visit Sweden's brochure *Fishing* from www.visit sweden.com.

Golf. Sweden has more than 300 golf courses. Most are private clubs, charging green fees, and some require visitors to have an official handicap. In the north during summertime you can enjoy the rare experience of playing golf under the midnight sun. Contact the Swedish Golf Federation (www.golf. se) for further information.

Horse riding. Riding is popular and most towns have stables and schools. There are many special treks for more experienced riders, ranging from day or weekend rides around Stockholm and Södermanland to mountain treks in Jämtland and Lappland, sometimes with hunting and fishing included. Local tourist offices can help you with arrangements.

Skiing. Swedes learn to ski as soon as they can walk. Sälen (in Dalarna; www.skistar.com) is the biggest skiing area: its seven resorts have 116 runs between them. Åre (in Jämtland; www.skistar.com) and Idre Fjäll (in Dalarna; www.idrefjall.se) are also extremely popular. All have downhill runs and miles of cross-country tracks.

Walking. In summer, walking is the Swede's preferred outdoor activity. The long-distance upland paths, such as Kungsleden in Lappland (see page 83), attract hundreds every weekend, yet never become crowded. There are also forest tracks and space where *allemansrätt,* the law that allows wandering at will,

Sweden is a hiker's paradise

can be enjoyed. You'll find mountain huts on most routes, and elsewhere wilderness camping is the attraction, especially in the National Parks.

Water sports. There are limitless possibilities, including canoeing, sailing, windsurfing, water-skiing, and white-water rafting (particularly in the north). In summer, lakes Vänern and Vättern are dotted with boats, swimmers and anglers. Every town has its indoor and/or outdoor swimming pool, and you can hire motor and sailing boats all over Sweden.

Winter activities. Between late November and March, tour skating (www.iceguide.se) is popular around the islands of the Stockholm archipelago. In the far north, many 'winter activities' are available all year round: drive a team of huskies, go snowmobiling, try ice-fishing, or slide a rally car across a frozen lake. See www.swedishlapland.com for a list of local tourist offices.

NATIONAL PARKS

Sweden's wild and lovely landscape is protected by 29 National Parks, spread throughout the country from Lappland to Skåne. The largest, **Padjelanta**, covers 198,400 hectares (some 490,250 acres) – a greater area than Lake Vänern. One or two parks – for example, the wild mountain terrain of **Sarek** in Lappland – are total wildernesses, where Swedes indulge their passion for getting back to nature, and where you can wander for days without seeing another soul.

Others have footpaths, walking trails, accommodation and even cable cars. **Sånjfället** in Härjedallen has a bear population, and on the island of **Blå Jungfrun**, in the Kalmar Sound in Småland, legend tells that witches appear on the night of Maundy Thursday before Easter. Further information is available from the Swedish Environmental Protection Agency (Naturvårdsverket; www.naturvardsverket.se; tel: 010-698 10

00) and the Swedish Touring Club (Svenska Turistföreningen, STF; www.svenskaturistforeningen.se; tel: 08-463 21 00).

The STF runs almost 400 youth hostels, mountain stations and mountain huts, which vary from basic shelters to hotel-standard places.

SHOPPING

The prices at high-class department stores like NK, Åhléns and PUB and the designer boutiques around Biblioteksgatan are not for the faint-hearted. Keep an eye out for signs saying *'rea'*, meaning sale, and check out high-street stores like H&M and Lindex. Sweden is renowned for its furniture and design, with stores like Asplund, DesignTorget, Svenskt Tenn and Lagerhaus showcasing distinctive quality homeware. For IKEA fans, its largest store worldwide is in Skärholmen, 15 minutes drive south of Stockholm.

Sweden has many beautiful national parks

MOMS, Sweden's version of VAT, is levied on most goods. It currently stands at around 25 percent, with exceptions on foodstuffs and some services, but non-EU residents can reclaim most of this by getting a Tax Free Form when making a purchase over SEK 200 at a participating shop, and taking it (along with the receipt) to the Tax Free desk at the airport on departure. Check www.globalblue.com.

WHERE TO SHOP

Each of the three main cities has its browsing area: Gamla Stan in Stockholm, the busy Avenyn in Gothenburg, and in Malmö a long, traffic-free zone that stretches along Södergatan from Stortorget. In addition, Gothenburg has popular Haga Nygata and the huge Nordstan shopping centre. Opened in Malmö in 2012, Emporia, is one of Scandinavia's largest shopping centres.

A design store in Gothenburg

Stockholm's colourful indoor **market halls include the city's oldest,** Östermalms Saluhall (www.ostermalms hallen.se; closed until 2018 for renovations, a temporary market hall is open at Östermalmstorg) and Hötorgshallen (www.hotorgshallen.se), both centrally located; and Söderhallarna (www.soderhallarna.se), on Medborgar-platsen in the bohemian district Södermalm. In Gothenburg, Feskekörka (http://feskekörka.se) was built as a church but is now a fish market, while Stora Saluhallen (market hall; www.storasaluhallen.se) at Kungstorget offers food stalls of all kinds. Many of Malmö's squares have market stalls, while the streets around Malmö's Möllevångstorget are good for cafés, delicatessens and groceries. Every week-end from June to September, Sweden's largest weekend **fleamarket**, Täbyloppis (www.tabyloppis.com) is held at Täby horse track (a 20-minute train ride away: get off at Galoppfältet).

WHAT TO BUY

Overall, your best bets are any of the following, reflecting Sweden's excellent design tradition. Also worth trying is Scandinavian chocolate, among the best anywhere.

Clothes. Both men and women's clothes are beautifully designed: think Anna Holtblad, Fifth Avenue Shoe Repair, Odd Molly or Nudie's must-have jeans. There are many boutiques where bargains can be found (especially during end-of-season sales), as well as more well-known stores like H&M and Filippa K.

Crafts. Svensk Hemslöjden stores are located throughout Sweden, and are the place to go for locally made clothing and handicrafts, normally at reasonable prices. Gold and silver are usually good, and if you spot the signs *guldsmed* or *silversmed,* you might also find original designs.

An open-air bar in Stockholm

Glass. The province of Småland is Sweden's 'Kingdom of Crystal' (see pages 50) and home to famous names such as Kosta Boda and Orrefors, as well as many smaller companies. In most of the glassworks you can pick up 'imperfect' items for less than half price. See www.glasriket.se for studio locations and deals.

Porcelain. This comes to the big stores direct from the picturesque Gustavsberg factory, Sweden's last-remaining porcelain producer, situated just outside Stockholm.

Textiles. These can be expensive, but cheaper items can sometimes be found in factories. A good place within driving distance of Gothenburg is Borås in *Tygriket* (Weaver's Country).

ENTERTAINMENT

For a country of just 9.8 million people, Sweden has a very proud tradition of the dramatic, musical and visual arts, both in the larger cities and the outlying areas.

CLASSICAL MUSIC, OPERA, BALLET AND JAZZ

Classical music, opera and ballet in Sweden compare with the best in the world. Theatre and concert performances usually run from late August to mid-June.

The Konserthuset (www.konserthuset.se) is the venue for performances by the **Stockholm Philharmonic Orchestra**, while the **Swedish Radio Symphony Orchestra** uses the Berwaldhallen (www.berwaldhallen.se) as a base. Gothenburg and Malmö also have Konserthusets, home to the

Gothenburg Symphony Orchestra (www.gso.se) and the **Malmö Symphony Orchestra** (www.mso.se) respectively.

All three cities have opera houses that stage opera and ballet performances, and sometimes musicals: Stockholm's **Royal Opera House** (Operan; www.operan.se), **Göteborgs-Operan** (www.opera.se) and **Malmö Opera** (www.malmo opera.se).

Music is frequently offered in lovely alternative settings: the **Royal Palace** and **Drottningholms Slottsteater** (www. kungahuset.se) in Stockholm and **Liseberg** (www.liseberg. se) in Gothenburg – not forgetting **Malmöhus** in Malmö. **Parkteatern** is a programme of concerts, theatre and other festivities that takes place in many city parks in July.

Scandinavians adore jazz and there are plenty of concerts and jazz festivals held in Sweden every year. Many of these take place in the colder months, such as Stockholm and

Jazz club in Stockholm

Gothenburg's Way Out West festival

Umeå jazz festivals, both held in October.

THEATRE AND CINEMA

For most visitors, language will prove a major problem at the theatre, as plays are usually performed in Swedish. Cinema is another matter, as almost all foreign films are shown in their original language with Swedish subtitles.

NIGHTLIFE

Swedes used to go home early. Today – in the cities at least – that's all changed, and clubs (some attached to the bigger hotels), dance restaurants and live venues may stay open to 3am, particularly on Friday and Saturday. The rural areas, however, offer little late-night entertainment except in hotels. Many nightclubs have minimum age restrictions as high as 23 or 25 – bring ID if you look younger.

The Stockholm Visitors Board publishes a guide to what is happening around the capital. Events and gigs are also listed on tourist office websites.

FESTIVALS

Swedes celebrate their festivals with zest. Though fewer attend church on Sundays than in days gone by, there is still a bedrock of traditional values.

Walpurgis Night and May Day *(Valborgsmässoafton och Första Maj)*. Bonfires blaze for Walpurgis Night on 30 April, giving this celebration of the end of the long, dark winter a truly pagan feel. In the old capital city of Uppsala, students 'sing in the spring' with traditional songs and speeches. In the evening the town is alight with torchlit parades and street parties. Rural areas are far more likely to celebrate May Day, with outdoor picnics, games and competitions.

National Day *(Svenska Nationaldagen)*. Swedes came late to the idea of a special National Day, but 6 June was chosen because the great Gustav Vasa, who founded the Vasa dynasty, became king on 6 June 1523. Nowadays, there are parades throughout the country, and the king and queen take part in a ceremony at Skansen open-air museum.

Midsummer *(Midsommar)*. This is by far the biggest summer celebration in Sweden; it was traditionally held on the solstice, but is now celebrated on the weekend nearest 24 June. Everywhere is decorated with flowers and greenery, and almost every community has its maypole; the dancing goes on long into the night. On this day, girls pick seven different flowers from as many places, and put them under their pillow to dream of their future husband. Skansen in Stockholm and Liseberg in Gothenburg are excellent places to join in. Sweden's national maypole is raised near Leksand in Dalarna.

It is tradition to raise a maypole for Midsummer

Lucia. The celebration of St Lucia, on 13 December, is Sweden's great winter feast,

Gröna Lund fun park in Stockholm

when communities around the country choose their own Lucia, who is dressed all in white with a crown of candles in her hair. Lucia is followed by a train of white-clad girls and boys, and brings in a tray of coffee, saffron rolls, ginger biscuits and *glögg* (mulled wine). Sweden's national Lucia is crowned at Skansen, and there are special Lucia concerts all over the country. The festival, like so many in Sweden, has much to do with light; the glitter and candles symbolise a belief that, however dark December is, the light will return.

The start of the **Crayfish and 'Sour Herring' season** *(Kräft och Surströmmingspremiären)* in August is another festival well worth noting (see page 105).

CHILDREN'S SWEDEN

Sweden is extremely child friendly, and all public transport facilities have pram access. Most cafés and restaurants have high-chairs, and staff are more than happy to heat food and bottles.

Many country hotels and camping sites have their own pools, plus sports and **play areas**. In addition, there are numerous public play areas called *Parklek,* which provide bikes and tricycles, buckets and spades, and other toys, as well as attendants and refreshments.

The two great **amusement parks** in Sweden are Gröna Lund in Stockholm and Liseberg in Gothenburg. In the capital there is also the **open-air museum**, Skansen, with its fascinating old buildings, aquarium and petting zoo, filled with baby animals over summer.

Junibacken (www.junibacken.se; Mar–Apr and Sept Tue–Sun 10am–5pm, rest of the year daily 10am–5pm, July–mid-Aug until 6pm), on Djurgården in Stockholm, is home to Astrid Lindgren's Pippi Longstocking and other storybook characters. The café serves great food.

SUMMER MUSIC FESTIVALS

Sweden's never-ending summer skies form a high blue canopy over the stages of some excellent music festivals.

June is a bumper month for rock and pop, with three of the biggest festivals – Peace & Love (www.peaceandlove.nu; in Borlänge), Hultsfredsfestivalen (www.hultsfredfestivalen.se) and the Sweden Rock Festival (www.swedenrock.com; in Sölvesborg) – coming to a field near you. June is also the month of the house and electronic festival Summerburst (www.summerburst.se; in Stockholm). Recently created but already very popular Bråvalla (www.bravallafestival.se) is located on the outskirts of Norrköping. Considered one of Europe's hottest festivals, Gothenburg's Way Out West (www.wayoutwest.se) is held in August. Dalhalla (www.dalhalla.se), a dramatic amphitheatre in the middle of a disused limestone quarry, hosts big-name rock, pop and opera stars from mid-June to September.

Opera buffs are treated to two picturesque castle backdrops with the Läckö Slottsopera (http://lackoslott.se/opera.aspx) and Vadstena Summer Opera Festival (www.vadstena-akademien.org), both in July.

There are various "fiddlers' meets" in summertime, when Swedish folkies congregate in rural areas to play and dance. The week-long Musik vid Siljan (www.musikvidsiljan.se) grew from one such gathering, and is now the granddaddy of them all.

For further details, see the Swedish Music Festivals website www.musikfestivaler.se, www.evenemang.se/festivaler, or contact local tourist offices.

Learning to ski in Sweden

The **Tekniskamuseet** (Technical Museum; www.tekniska museet.se; daily 10am–5pm, Wed until 8pm) in Stockholm is fascinating for older children and covers Swedish science and technology through the ages. **Tom Tits Experiment** (www.tomtit.se) hands-on science museum, located in Södertalje (30km/19 miles south of Stockholm), is a must.

Gothenburg's **Universeum** (www.universeum.se) is a pretty spectacular science centre/aquarium/tropical world; and kids will love exploring tugs, barges and battleships at **Maritiman** (www.maritiman.se).

Some historic buildings have their own children's sections, including **Läckö** (www.lackoslott.se), north of Lidköping on Lake Vänern, and **Tidö Slott** (www.tidoslott.se), north of Mälaren, which has a huge collection of dolls and toys. Around 130km (80 miles) south of Stockholm, in Södermanland, is **Kolmården Wild Animal Park** (www.kolmarden.com), with a pets' corner and creatures including tigers, gorillas and dolphins.

Over on the east coast, **Astrid Lindgrens Värld** (www.alv.se) in Vimmerby is a celebration of the works of the popular children's writer. Scandinavia's largest water park, **Sommarland** (www.sommarland.se), is in nearby Skara.

In the north, there are three different **zoos** at Östersund, Junsele and Lycksele, and unusual museums, such as the **Teknikens Hus** (Technical House; www.teknikenshus.se) in Luleå, which keeps kids occupied with hands-on exhibitions.

CALENDAR OF EVENTS

February: Jokkmokk Sami Market (Norrland), held since 1605.
March: International Horse Show (Gothenburg).
Vasaloppet cross-country ski race.
30 April/1 May: Walpurgis Night celebrations, followed by May Day/Labour Day festivities.
June: Midsummer. Bonfires and maypole dancing.
National Day on 6 June, marked with parades.
Archipelago Boat Day (Stockholm): vintage boats sail to Vaxholm.
Stockholm Marathon.
Sweden Rock Festival (Sölvesborg).
Vätternrundan (Motala) bicycle ride (300km/186 miles).
Hultsfredsfestivalen (Småland): big-name rock and pop bash.
Peace & Love Festival (Borlänge, Dalarna): Sweden's biggest music festival.
Round Gotland Race (Sandhamn): classic offshore regatta.
July: Music vid Siljan: folk and jazz around Lake Siljan.
Swedish Tennis Open (Båstad).
Gothia Cup (Gothenburg): youth soccer tournament (1,600 teams).
Falsterbo Horse Show.
Storsjöyran Festival (Östersund): international music festival.
August: Stockholm Pride, Scandinavia's largest gay-pride event.
Medieval Week (Visby), with costumed events.
Crayfish and 'Sour Herring' season begins.
Way Out West (Gothenburg): two-day music festival.
Stockholm & Gothenburg Culture Festivals: free music, art and drama.
Karl-Oskardagarna (Vaxjö): remembering Småland's emigrants.
Malmö Festival.
September: Swedish Derby (Malmö).
October: Lidingöloppet (Stockholm), cross-country race.
Stockholm and Umeå Jazz Festivals.
December: Nobel Prize Day (Stockholm) on 10 December.
St Lucia Festival, 13 December.

EATING OUT

Swedish restaurants have undergone a revolution in the last two decades. Today Sweden's top chefs make fabulous use of the country's clean flavours and natural produce, from the smoky tang of reindeer, boar and grouse, to North-Sea salmon and lobster, to the sweet piquancy of summer fruits. New settlers have brought new cuisines, and Stockholm, Gothenburg and Malmö contain a good range of ethnic food shops and restaurants. Choice is more limited in rural areas, where hotels, inns and manor houses tend to serve the best Swedish fare.

WHEN TO EAT

On the whole, Swedes eat earlier than other nations. Hotel breakfasts *(frukost)* are a less lavish version of the *smörgåsbord* cold table (see page 102), and will keep you going for most of the day. Lunch is served from 11am – look out for places serving the good-value *dagens rätt* (set lunch menu, Monday to Friday). Evening meals are generally served at 6pm, although many bigger restaurants and hotels expect their guests to arrive later. Restaurants are often closed on Sundays, and many shut down in July.

WHERE TO EAT

Eighteen restaurants in Stockholm, Gothenburg and Malmö have Michelin stars, and Malmö also has more restaurants per head than anywhere else in Sweden. In all three cities, top-class places often view expense-account diners as their primary clientele and can be expensive. However, there are a growing number of smaller, less pricey places, especially for lunch.

For street food, try one of the many *korvkiosk*. These covered food stalls serve plain but good fare: go for the Swedish favourite *korv* (sausage) in *tunnbröd*, flat bread filled with mashed potato, pickles and lettuce. Picnickers should visit the cities' market halls, in particular Stockholm's atmospheric Östermalmshallen (closed until 2018 for renovations, but you may visit a temporary market hall at Östermalmstorg), where delicatessen stalls loaded with meat, cheese, fish and cakes are complemented by good cafés and restaurants.

WHAT TO EAT

The Swedes like the natural products of river and forest, particularly fish and meats such as venison and reindeer. One food typical of midsummer is herring, which is often followed by a heap of fresh wild berries. Boiled potatoes arrive with most meals, usually sprinkled with dill.

Café in Stortorget in Stockholm

HUSMANSKOST

Traditional Swedish dishes are known by the general term *husmanskost* (home cooking). Sample them in retro style in rural areas, or with a modern twist in Stockholm's top restaurants. Two typical dishes, which hark back to the days when nothing was allowed to go to waste, are *Janssons Frestelse* (Jansson's Temptation), a tangy mixture of potato, onion and anchovy; and *pyttipanna* (literally, 'put in the pan'), a delicious fried-up hodgepodge of minced meat and other leftovers. *Köttbullar* (meatballs) and small sausages never go out of style; nor does *gravad lax*, delicately marinated salmon that is always served with a dill sauce.

SMÖRGÅSBORD

People all over the world use the word *smörgåsbord*, which originated in Sweden but is now found across Scandinavia. The direct translation ('sandwich table') fails to convey the art and majesty of this great buffet spread, which is a substantial, celebratory meal served on Sundays and special occasions.

It starts with herring of various sorts, shrimp, salmon and other fish. Next come the cold meats and cheeses, with caviar, eggs and different salads. This is followed by hot dishes, even though it is a 'cold' table, with fruit or pudding and coffee to follow. The traditional farming area of Skåne in the south claims to make the best *smörgåsbord*. Hotel breakfasts are often a smaller version of the meal.

FRUITS OF THE FOREST

The country's forests provide mushrooms (*svamp*) and wild berries, which *allemansrätt* (see page 118) allows you to pick anywhere; it is almost fashionable to return with stained fingers after a summer weekend. A profusion of wild berries grows in Scandinavia, from *smultron* (wild strawberries) to *hjortron* (cloudberries).

Traditional Swedish cinnamon buns (kanelbulle)

COFFEE AND CAKE

One of Sweden's finest traditions is the fika, an extended coffee break involving (at its very best) a cosy old *konditori*, a good gossip and a big cinnamon bun (*kanelbulle*). *Våfflor* (waffles), introduced to North America by Scandinavian emigrants, are available everywhere – consume with

Caviar is an essential part of the smörgåsbord

lashings of cream and jam. *Semlor,* once a traditional Shrove Tuesday delight eaten before the long fast, is now popular enough to appear immediately after Christmas. With a filling of almond paste and whipped cream, the buns are correctly served in a dish of hot milk with a sprinkling of cinnamon.

REGIONAL SPECIALITIES

The Skanska Matupplevelser (http://matupplevelser.skane.org) restaurant network promotes Skåne produce, like fresh asparagus, nutty new potatoes and handmade cheeses. Gothenburg is rated for its seafood: delicacies such as lobster and langoustine come into season in autumn. Gotland menus flaunt truffles and lamb, while people make the pilgrimage to Öland especially for its harvest vegetables. Norrland offers some of the choicest nibbles: feast on golden cloudberries, succulent arctic char, Västerbotten cheese, or rarities like ptarmigan (game bird).

If you're visiting Småland and the 'Kingdom of Crystal', look out for traditional **Hyttsill Evenings**. These hark back to the

Pickled herring is an enduring favourite

days when the glass-blowing hall was a social as well as a work place, and locals cooked herring beside the glowing furnaces. Pudding is the classic Småland delicacy, curd cake with sour cherry or strawberry jam, eaten to the sound of traditional music and storytelling.

DRINKS

Three beer strengths are available in restaurants: light (under 2.25 percent alcohol), ordinary (2.25–3.5 percent) and export (over 3.5 percent). 'Craft' beers are increasing in popularity, such as those from the prize-winning Nils Oscar microbrewery (Nyköping). You can purchase a cheap bottle of wine for around SEK 60 in the state alcohol stores, *Systembolaget* (www.systembolaget.se), but restaurants multiply that by three or more in an effort, so some say, to keep beer and spirit prices more reasonable. Aquavit is a must with herring at the start of the *smörgåsbord*.

AQUAVIT

Scandinavia's favourite firewater is Aquavit (*Akvavit*) – the water of life – which is also sometimes called *snaps*. Sweden's most popular brand is *Skåne*.

Straight aquavit is distilled from potatoes or barley. What makes each brand different is what goes into it afterwards – usually dill or caraway, followed by whatever distinctive flavours the distiller can devise.

Aquavit is served in tiny glasses and quaffed ice cold (many families cool it in the freezer, or in the snow outside). It is drunk at the beginning of a meal, usually as an accompaniment to fish – ideally the herring that starts a *smörgåsbord.* Raising your glass in a toast is an essential part of the ancient ritual.

Many Swedes experiment with their own flavours, putting a leaf or sprig of herbs into a half bottle and leaving it to mature. Home distilling is an open secret: if you're offered a selection of aquavit in a private house, don't enquire about the brand!

THE CRAYFISH AND 'SOUR HERRING' SEASON

Swedes have an understandable passion for crayfish and – to those not born to it – an inexplicable taste for *surströmming* (fermented herring), which replaces crayfish further north.

The crayfish season starts in August with a grand outdoor party. Sporting comic hats and paper bibs, guests sit at a long table lit by paper lanterns and loaded with glasses, aquavit and delicious crayfish. Eating is punctuated by toasts, traditional songs and toasting songs, including the best known of all, *Helan går...* (something equivalent to 'down in one'), the intricacies of which are better attempted than explained.

Surströmming is a dish made of Baltic herring, salted, set aside for a long time, then canned. It continues to ferment until its tin bulges ominously, and is opened with great caution (usually outdoors and/or underwater). The brave eat it with *tunnbröd* (thin bread), raw onions and *mandelpotatis* (small, sweetish, almondshaped potatoes). Connoisseurs claim that milk is the correct drink. To many Swedes – and all foreigners – the downing of this overpowering meal is something of a test of machismo.

TO HELP YOU ORDER ...

May I have the menu, please? **Kan jag få matsedeln, tack?**

What do you recommend? **Vad rekommenderar ni?**

Do you have any vegetarian dishes? **Har ni några vegetariska rätter?**

I'd like to pay. **Får jag betala.**

beetroot **rödbetor**	prawns **räkor**
carrots **morötter**	reindeer **ren**
cauliflower **blomkål**	roast beef **rostbiff**
chicken **kyckling**	roast lamb **lammstek**
egg dishes **äggrätter**	salmon **lax**
ham **skinka**	smoked Baltic herring **buckling**
mushrooms **svamp**	
octopus **bläckfisk**	spinach **spenat**
onions **lök**	tea **te**
orange **äppelsin**	tomatoes **tomater**
peas **ärtor**	trout **forell**
pike **gädda**	tuna **tonfisk**
pork chop **fläskkotlett**	venison **rådjur**

... AND READ THE MENU

bakverk pastries	**ost** cheese
drycker drinks	**pastarätter** pasta
efterrätter desserts	**risrätter** rice
fågel poultry	**sallader** salad
fisk fish	**skaldjur** seafood
förrätter starters	**soppor** soups
från grillen grilled (broiled)	**smårätter** snacks
frukt fruit	**smörgåsar** sandwiches
glass ice-cream	**smorgasbord** cold table
grönsaker vegetables	**varmrätter** main course
huvudrätter main course	**vilt** game
kött meat	**vinlista** wine list

PLACES TO EAT

Prices are for an evening meal for two, without wine.

$$$$** Over SEK 1,000 **$$$ SEK 550–1,000
$$** SEK 350–550   **$ Below SEK 350

STOCKHOLM

Berns Asiatiska $$$–$$$$ *Berzelli Park, tel: 08-566 322 00,* www.
berns.se. The superb 19th-century surroundings are so fab that you
may not notice the food! There's an extensive menu at this upmarket
Asian brasserie, popular for its weekend brunch. Open daily.

Blå Porten Café $ *Djurgårdsvägen 64; tel: 08-663 87 59;* www.bla
porten.com. This attractive restaurant is in a former art gallery,
with a pretty, central garden. Good, simple food, with an emphasis
on Swedish cuisine. Open Mon, Wed, Fri, Sun 11am–7pm, Tue, Thu
11am–9pm, Sat 11am–8pm.

Fem Små Hus $$$–$$$$ *Nygränd 10; tel: 08-10 87 75;* www.femsma
hus.se. This classic Stockholm restaurant, in vaulted cellars near
the Royal Palace, offers fantastic Swedish cooking and old-time
charm. Beautifully prepared dishes include filet of reindeer with
cranberries and port wine sauce, oven-baked salmon with white-
wine sauce and delicious berry desserts. Open daily from 5pm.

Grill $$$ *Drottninggatan 89; tel: 08-31 45 30;* www.grill.se. This place
is fun, stylish and a little eccentric. The grilled dishes (with a sepa-
rate vegetarian menu) span a number of ethnic cuisines. Open lunch
Mon–Fri, dinner daily.

Hasselbacken $$$ *Hazeliusbacken 20; tel: 08-517 343 07;* www.
restauranghasselbacken.com. Famous 19th-century restaurant
with a large terrace garden. Enjoy international and traditional
Swedish food in a beautiful setting. Open breakfast daily, brunch
Sat–Sun, lunch Mon–Fri, dinner Mon–Sat.

Hermans $ *Fjällgatan 23; tel: 08-643 94 80;* www.hermans.se. A
highly popular international vegetarian buffet restaurant, Her-

mans offers fantastic views over Stockholm. Live bands in summer. Open daily 11am–9pm.

Mathias Dahlgren $$$$ *Södra Blasieholmshamnen 6; tel: 08-679 35 84; www.mdghs.com.* Bocuse d'Or-winner Mathias Dahlgren has earned three Michelin stars for his two restaurants at the Grand Hôtel. Both serve superb Swedish-inspired food complemented with exceptional wines: Matsalen (open dinner Tue–Sat) is the more exclusive venue, while Matbaren (open lunch Mon–Fri, dinner Mon–Sat) is a more relaxed bistro, with seats around the bar for drop-in diners.

Operakällarens Matsal $$$$ *Operahuset, Karl XIIs Torg; tel: 08-676 58 01; www.operakallaren.se.* A venerable institution (over 200 years old), with astonishing 19th-century decor, Operakällaren serves French haute-cuisine, with the occasional nod to Swedish culinary tradition. Open Tue–Sat dinner.

Pelikan $$-$$$ *Blekingegatan 40; tel: 08-556 09 090; www.pelikan. se.* A Stockholm institution, this bar-restaurant has been going for well over a century. Food is traditional Swedish (meatballs, veal schnitzel, and 'SOS' – or 'smör, ost, sill'), served in a high-ceilinged hall. Open lunch Fri–Sun, dinner daily.

Pubologi $$$-$$$$ *Stora Nygatan 20, Gamla Stan; tel: 08-506 400 86; www.pubologi.se.* This trendy gastropub, where diners share one large table, has won accolades galore. The menu has a strong Mediterranean influence, and half portions are the norm so you get to try two or three flavour-packed dishes. Open dinner Mon–Sat.

MALMÖ AND THE SOUTH

MALMÖ

Årstiderna $$$-$$$$ *Frans Suellsgatan 3; tel: 040-23 09 10; www. arstiderna.se.* Sample Swedish and international cooking in an exclusive vaulted 16th-century building. Closed Sun.

Atmosfär $$$ *Fersens Väg 4; tel: 040-12 50 77; www.atmosfar. com.* This stunning restaurant serves beautifully presented Skåne dishes with a fresh, modern twist. The great wine list rounds things off nicely. Closed Sun.

Bloom in the Park $$$ *Pildammsvägen 2; tel: 040-793 63;* www. bloominthepark.se. Situated in Pildammsparken, this elegant restaurant throws away the menu and concentrates on delivering deliciously experimental gourmet dishes – it's a memorable dining experience. Open lunch by appointment only, dinner Mon–Sat, afternoon tea Sun.

Johan P $$ *Saluhallen, Lilla Torg; tel: 040-97 18 18;* www.johanp.nu. In Malmö's market hall, Johan P is considered the best place in Malmö for fish, brought straight from the sea each morning. Open lunch and dinner daily.

Mrs Brown $$$ *Storgatan 26; tel: 040-97 22 50;* www.mrsbrown. nu. An understandably popular spot, the focus here is firmly on seasonal Skåne ingredients: think smoked lamb, juicy homemade sausages, sweet new potatoes and gingery rhubarb. Open dinner Mon–Sat.

Mrs Saigon $$ *Engelbrektsgatan 17; tel: 040-788 35;* www.mrs-saigon.se. Crowds descend on this Vietnamese place at lunchtime for the good-value hot buffet. The evening menu is more traditional, offering dishes such as succulent tiger prawns, Vietnamese pancakes and spicy beef in sweet soybean sauce. Open lunch Mon–Sat, dinner Tue–Sat.

Salt & Brygga $$–$$$ *Sundspromenaden 7; tel: 040-611 59 40;* www.saltobrygga.se. This place subscribes to an eco-friendly concept – from the furnishings to the cooking – and serves innovative international cuisine. It's near the Turning Torso, with outdoor summer seating and magnificent views of Öresund. Open Mon–Fri 11.30am–11pm, Sat noon–11pm, Sun noon–10pm.

Tempo Bar & Kök $$–$$$ *Södra Skolgatan 30; tel: 040-12 60 21;* www.tempobarokok.se. In a great location close to Möllevångstorget, this trendy restaurant serves international dishes and has a lively and popular bar. Open Mon–Sat dinner.

SKÅNE

Brösarps Gästgifveri $$ *Albovägen 21, Brösarp; tel: 0414-736 80;* www.brosarpsgastgifveri.se. Authentic Skåne dishes made from locally grown produce are served in a beautiful 16th-century inn in Brösarp village (about 30km north of Ystad). Open lunch and dinner daily, phone for dinner reservations.

Mat & Destillat $$$ *Kyrkogatan 17, Lund; tel: 0461-28 000;* http://matochdestillat.se. Don't miss this popular restaurant if you are in Lund. High-quality, traditional Swedish dishes are on the expensive side here, but are well worth the money. Open for lunch and dinner.

Upp eller Ner $$ *Stortorget 11, Ystad; tel: 0411-78 800;* www.uppellerner.se. A popular pub-cum-restaurant in the very heart of Ystad. Great for drinks and/or an evening meal. Open Mon–Sat from 5pm till late.

BALTIC ISLANDS

Bakfickan $$$ *Stora Torget 1, Visby, Gotland; tel: 0498-27 18 07;* http://bakfickanvisby.se. Beautiful fresh seafood (scallops, fried herring, char with quails' eggs) is served in this bustling little place, always packed with locals. It's in Visby, by Sankta Karins church. Open daily lunch and dinner.

Hotell Borgholm $$$–$$$$ *Trädgårdsgatan 15-19, Borgholm, Öland; tel: 0485-770 60;* www.hotellborgholm.com. The finest food on Öland. Fresh, flavour-packed dishes include cod with cider broth and Öland truffles, or malt-roast duck with raspberry coulis. Open Mar–Aug Mon–Sat dinner, Sept–Dec Tue–Sat dinner.

GOTHENBURG AND THE WEST

GOTHENBURG

Café Husaren $ *Haga Nygata 28; tel: 031-13 63 78;* www.cafehusaren.se. This cosy café in the historic Haga district bakes the world's largest kanelbullar (cinnamon buns). Open daily until 6pm, Mon–Thu until 8pm.

Caleo $$$ *Engelbrektsgatan 39B; tel: 031-708 93 40; www.caleo. se.* This long-standing local favourite has recently had a re-vamp: high-class, beautifully presented Mediterranean food is now served in a sleek, modern setting. Open for dinner daily. No reservations – get there early.

Heaven 23 $$$–$$$$ *Hotel Gothia Towers; tel: 031-750 88 05; www.heaven23.se.* This trendy gourmet restaurant on the 23rd floor of Gothia Towers offers awesome views over the city. The great cocktails are complemented by DJs on Friday and Satur-day nights. Open lunch and dinner daily.

Hello Monkey $$$ *Magasinsgatan 26; tel: 031-13 04 42; www. hellomonkey.net.* This quirky restaurant, with its monkey-based decor and open kitchen, serves an Asian-Australian menu including tasty sashimi and dim sum. Open for dinner Tue–Sun.

Kock & Vin $$$$ *Viktoriagatan 12; tel: 031-701 79 79; www. kockvin.se.* A Michelin-starred restaurant, Kock & Vin offers Swedish-inspired gastronomic cuisine: tiny, intense dishes served on plates, pebbles and driftwood. Downstairs is the more laidback Björns bar-restaurant. Open for dinner Mon–Sat. Closed July.

M2 – Magnus & Magnus $$$ *Magasinsgatan 8; tel: 031-13 30 00; www.magnusmagnus.se.* A cosy restaurant with a rather ro-mantic candlelit courtyard, which is a favourite summer eating place. You can choose between the 2-, 3-, and 4-course menus available. It's good value for such high-quality food. Open for dinner daily.

Park Aveny Café $$$ *Elite Park Avenue Hotel, Kungsportsave-nyn 36-38; tel: 031-727 10 76; www.parkavenycafe.se.* A Goth-enburg institution, this well-heeled hotel brasserie serves French bistro food in a great setting along the main boulevard. It also puts on a well-attended Sunday brunch.

Restaurang 28+ $$$–$$$$ *Götabergsgatan 28; tel: 031-20 21 61;* www.28plus.se. This exclusive, Michelin-starred restaurant has the city's best wine cellar. Most people opt for the 5- or 7-course tasting menus. Open dinner Mon–Sat. Closed July–Aug.

Restaurang Solrosen $ *Kaponjärgatan 4A; tel: 031-711 66 97;* www. restaurangsolrosen.se. A friendly, good-value vegetarian restaurant offering a tasty buffet of soup, salad and three veggie/vegan mains. Closed Sun July–Aug.

Restaurang Tvåkanten $$$ *Kungportsavenyn 27; tel: 031-18 21 15;* www.tvakanten.se. Enjoy modern food in beautiful old premises. The Sunday roast dinner is popular. Open lunch Tue–Fri, dinner daily.

GÖTA KANAL

Vadstena Valven $$ *Storgatan 18, Vadstena; tel: 0143-123 40;* www. valven.se. This beautiful, historic building is home to some good traditional and international dishes, made using local ingredients. Open daily for lunch and dinner.

HALMSTAD

Pio Matsal & Bar $$$ *Storgatan 37; tel: 035-21 06 69;* www.pio. se. Traditional Swedish food is presented in a contemporary style. The venue lays on some great tasting nights: check ahead for upcoming events. Open for dinner daily.

THE CENTRAL HEARTLANDS

ÅRE

Villa Tottebo $$$$ *Parkvägen 1; tel: 0647-506 20;* www.villa tottebo.se. Sweden's top ski resort has plenty of stylish restaurants, including Villa Tottebo, cuddled into a cosy 19th-century hunting lodge. It serves traditional Jämtland dishes, based on native ingredients: fresh venison, mountain lamb and cloudberries. Open for dinner daily.

DALARNA

Vårdhuset Dala-Floda $$ *Badvägen 6, Dala-Floda; tel: 0241-220 50;* www.dalafloda-vardshus.se. A delightful, beautifully decorated inn with an excellent restaurant serving local and international dishes. Both restaurant and hotel are certified organic. Reservations necessary. Open June–Aug lunch daily, Sept–May by reservation, dinner.

ÖSTERSUND

Brunkullans Krog $$ *Postgränd 5; tel: 063-10 14 54;* http://brunkullan brasserie.se. This charming little restaurant in one of the old quarters of Östersund offers international and traditional Swedish dishes. Try the comfortable bar if you're just after a drink. Open lunch Mon–Fri, dinner Tue–Sat.

NORRLAND AND THE ARCTIC

UMEÅ

Rex Bar & Grill $$–$$$ *Rådhustorget; tel: 090-70 60 50;* www. rexbar.com. A stylish, trendy bar and restaurant serving French-influenced bistro food. Closed Sun.

GAMMELSTAD (LULEÅ)

Margaretas Värdshus $$$ *Lulevägen 2; tel: 0920-25 42 90;* www. margaretasvardshus.se. A picturesque inn, with an award-winning restaurant serving mainly regional dishes (reindeer, ptarmigan, arctic char). Phone for opening times.

KIRUNA

Icehotel Restaurant $$$$ *Marknadsvägen; tel: 0980-66 800;* www. icehotel.com. Award-winning New Nordic gastronomy from locally sourced ingredients. Pure ice sorbets from the River Torneto cleanse the palate between courses. The company also runs the relaxed Old Homestead restaurant. Icehotel opens Dec–mid-Apr for lunch and for dinner daily, Old Homestead dinner daily.

A–Z TRAVEL TIPS

A Summary of Practical Information

A

ACCOMMODATION (*logi*; see also CAMPING, YOUTH HOSTELS and the list of RECOMMENDED HOTELS starting on page 136)

Swedish hotels (*hotell*) are almost invariably warm, comfortable and well run. Many higher-grade hotels have saunas and plunge pools and some also have swimming pools. They are also among Europe's higher-priced hotels, and the secret to keeping costs reasonable is to choose the time you visit Sweden. Hotels are geared to business travel, and during slack periods (generally mid-June to mid-August and at weekends) they slash their rates (sometimes by as much as 50 percent). Always ask about discounts and special rates, including the special Stockholm, Gothenburg and Malmö packages. The largest hotel chain in Sweden and the Nordic region is Scandic Hotels (www.scandichotels.com); children under 12 stay for free.

Before making plans, check out www.visitsweden.com for accommodation advice and online booking.

Self-catering accommodation is also good. A Swedish family may rent out its own *stuga* (traditional wooden holiday house). Tour operators and tourist offices offer self-catering packages and there are more than 350 purpose-built holiday villages, with canoes, bikes, boats, etc for hire. Around 250 working farms offer farmstay accommodation – see the Bo på Lantgård (Stay on a Farm) website (www.bopalantgard.org) for listings.

AIRPORTS (*flygplatser*)

Sweden's two busiest international airports are Arlanda (Stockholm) and Göteborg-Landvetter (Gothenburg). Budget airlines also use Stockholm-Skavsta and Stockholm-Vasterås airports; and there are limited direct flights to Malmö. All have airport coaches (*Flygbussarna*) to and from their respective city's central station. Taxis are more expensive: from Arlanda, Taxi 020, Taxi Kurir and

Taxi Stockholm offer fixed fares into the city centre that are usually cheaper than a metered ride, especially at rush hour.

Arlanda (ARN; tel: 010-109 10 00; www.arlanda.se) is 42km (26 miles) north of Stockholm centre, and 36km (22 miles) southeast of Uppsala. For Stockholm, the fastest way to/from the airport is via the ArlandaExpress (return SEK 530; www.arlandaexpress.com), a high-speed train that departs every 15 minutes for the 20-minute trip. The airport coach (return SEK 198; www.airshuttle.se) makes several stops in the outer suburbs before terminating at Stockholm's central railway station. Cheaper/slower bus and train services are also available. For Uppsala, trains leave every 30 minutes and bus no. 801 departs hourly.

Cheap airlines, including Ryanair, fly into both **Stockholm-Skavsta** (NYO; tel: 0155-280 400; www.skavsta.se) and **Stockholm-Vasterås** (VST; tel: 021-805 600; www.stockholmvasteras.se) airports, both about 100km (62 miles) from Stockholm. Local buses and hourly airport coaches serve both airports, with the journey to Stockholm taking 1.5 hours.

Göteborg-Landvetter (GOT; tel: 010-10 93 100; www.swedavia. se/landvetter) is 24km (17 miles) east of Gothenburg. The airport coach takes around 20 minutes to and from the centre.

Malmö-Sturup (MMX; tel: 010-10 945 00; www.swedavia.se/malmo) is 30km (21 miles) southeast of the city centre (40 to 50 minutes).

B

BICYCLE RENTAL

Sweden's uncrowded roads make cycling popular, and bicycles can be rented almost anywhere; the local tourist office usually has details. Typical cost: SEK 180 per day. Maps and bike route suggestions are available from most tourist offices. Stockholm and Gothenburg also operate public city-bike schemes. Visit www.city bikes.se and www.goteborgbikes.se for more information.

BUDGETING FOR YOUR TRIP

All prices given are approximate. Stockholm is usually the most expensive location.

Accommodation. A bed in a youth-hostel dorm costs around SEK 200/250 for members/non-members. Average rates for hotels vary considerably. Hotel prices drop considerably with special weekend and summer rates and packages. *(See also* Accommodation and the list of Recommended Hotels *starting on page* 136).

Meals and drinks. Good-value lunchtime specials (SEK 70–100) are served weekdays and comprise salad, a main course and coffee – look for the sign *Dagens rätt* (dish of the day). A three-course dinner at a medium-priced restaurant (not including drinks) costs around SEK 400 per head, coffee or soft drinks SEK 28, a bottle of wine in a restaurant SEK 450 and up, a bottle of beer from SEK 45, a shot of spirits SEK 30. Food and (especially) alcoholic drinks are expensive.

Museums. SEK 40–150, average SEK 100. Under 18s often get in free.

Public transport. In Stockholm a single bus, *Tunnelbana* or local train ticket for zones 1/2/3 costs SEK 36/54/72. Note: travel on Stockholm's buses is free for one parent accompanying a child in a pushchair – board through the exit door (www.sl.se).

Taxis. Charges vary according to the time of day, but it should not cost more than SEK 300 for a 10km/15-minute journey.

Tourist City Cards. Stockholm, Gothenburg and Malmö all have concessionary cards, with big savings on sightseeing, public transport and shopping, bought from tourist information centres. To purchase online, visit www.mystockholmpass.com and www.goteborg.com. Stockholm Pass gives free tours by bus or boat, free travel on Hop On – Hop Off buses and boat, free entry to selected museums and attractions, and discounts in restaurants and shops. A 1-/2-/3-/4-day card costs SEK 545/645/765/890.

Trains: A single journey on the SJ high-speed service between Stockholm and Gothenburg, second class, costs SEK 145–600, depending on availability.

CAMPING *(camping)*

There are more than 500 camping sites, often by lake or sea, with boats, canoes and bikes for hire, and maybe riding, mini-golf and tennis on offer. As well as tent pitches, many sites also have two- to six-bed log cabins equipped with cooking facilities and utensils (but not bedding – bring sleeping bags). Most campsites are open in June–August, some earlier but not necessarily with full facilities. In skiing areas, some sites hire out their caravans in the depths of winter.

A membership card is required at the majority of Swedish camp-sites; the most widely accepted card is the Camping Key Europe (available online and at campsites for SEK 150). The website www.camping.se has useful information and an online booking service. The Camping Key Europe card can also be purchased here.

Sweden's access tradition *allemansrätt* (the right of public access) allows you one night's camping anywhere, without permission, except for private plots of land, but campers should not stay too close to houses, damage their surroundings or leave litter.

CAR HIRE *(biluthyrning;* see also BUDGETING FOR YOUR TRIP, DRIVING and MONEY)

Most big companies, such as Avis (tel: 0770-82 00 82; www.avis.se), Hertz (tel: 0771-211 212; www.hertz.se), Budget (tel: 0770-11 00 12; www.budget.se), Europcar (tel: 0770-77 00 50; www.europcar.se) and Sixt (tel: 010-20 90 800; http://se.sixt.com) have offices in airports and larger towns, with a wide range of cars. A small car (Ford Focus) for a week costs upwards of SEK 2,000, and a large estate car (Volvo V70) costs SEK 5,000, including tax, fees, collision damage waiver and theft protection. Special rates are usually available between mid-June and mid-August and weekends throughout the year. Always ask about discounts, particularly packages connected with domestic air and rail travel. You can often rent a car in one place and return it to another.

Most companies ask for a deposit, which is usually a credit card imprint. The legal minimum driving age in Sweden is 18, but to hire a car you usually need to have held a licence for three years, so in practice the minimum age is around 21.

CLIMATE

Shorts and T-shirts are often the norm in Stockholm during the summer, when temperatures well above 20°C (70°F) are common. The far north experiences average temperatures of 16°C (61°F) in summer, thanks to long hours of sunlight (up to 24 hours in July). Swimsuit skiing on the border at Björkliden, near Riksgränsen, is not unknown. Conversely, in the depths of winter, temperatures in the north can sink lower than -30°C (-22°F), while Stockholm usually shivers at just a couple of degrees below freezing.

The following chart shows the average daily maximum and minimum temperatures and number of rainy days each month in Stockholm.

	J	F	M	A	M	J	J	A	S	O	N	D
Max °F	31	31	37	45	57	65	70	66	58	48	38	33
Max °C	-1	-1	3	7	14	18	21	19	14	9	3	1
Min °F	23	22	26	32	41	49	55	53	46	39	31	26
Min °C	-5	-6	-3	0	5	9	13	12	8	4	-1	-3
Days of rainfall	10	7	6	7	7	8	7	10	9	9	10	11

CLOTHING

It is a good idea to be prepared for changes and to wear several layers. Even in summer keep a sweater and waterproof covering

to hand, as well as casual summer clothes. The north always de-
mands warm outerwear.

Winter also calls for layers. Houses are warm and the custom is
to leave heavy clothing just inside the front door (or in your hotel
cloakroom). Shoes are never worn inside houses. Walkers should
take good walking boots and a rucksack. Winter essentials are
warm headgear, and two pairs of gloves or mitts (one thin, one
thick). Good footwear is necessary for snow and slushy streets. If
you plan to be out of doors a lot, a thermal layer is advised. For
evenings, Swedes dress informally, casual but smart.

CRIME AND SAFETY (See also EMERGENCIES and POLICE)

Sweden is one of the safest countries in the world. It is usually safe
to walk in cities at night, but on Friday and Saturday evenings you
may meet groups of revellers – who are likely to be noisy rather
than dangerous – and Stockholm's *Tunnelbana* (underground) can
be boisterous. You may prefer a taxi. Should anything happen to
you, contact the police. The emergency number **112** is free when
called from payphones.

D

DISABLED TRAVELLERS

Facilities for people with disabilities include access ramps, lifts
and hotel rooms adapted for people with mobility difficulties or
allergies, good public transport access and special provisions for
swimming and riding. Almost all pedestrian crossings use sound to
indicate when it is safe to cross. For further information contact De
Handikappades Riksförbund (DHR), Storforsplan 44, 123 21 Farsta;
tel: 08-685 80 00; http://dhr.se.

DRIVING (See also CAR HIRE)

Swedish roads are well maintained and uncrowded; outside the cities driving is easy, despite the small number of motorways.

Speed limits. Speed limits, shown on road signs, are usually 50km/h (30mph) in built-up areas; 70km/h (43mph) on trunk roads; and 90 or 110km/h (55 or 70mph) on motorways. Caravan limits are lower, with a maximum of 80km/h (50mph).

Documents. To drive your own car in Sweden you need a national or international driving licence and valid third-party (or comprehensive) insurance. Vehicles not registered in Sweden must display a nationality sign.

Driving rules. Drive on the right, pass on the left. Note that Sweden has a 'right-hand rule' traffic law: if there is no sign indicating that you are on a *'huvudled'* (main road), and no give-way signs at an intersection, then you must always give way to traffic coming from road intersections to your right. (However, on a roundabout, give way to traffic entering from the left.) The use of seatbelts is obligatory for everyone in the car. Dipped headlights (which should be adjusted on right-hand-drive cars) must be used both day and night.

Drink-driving attracts very high fines, or even a jail sentence. The alcohol limit is 0.2 milligrams per litre of blood. The best course is never to drink if you're driving. Swedish police carry out frequent spot checks on licences and vehicles.

Note that a Swedish mile is equal to 10km; many Swedes are unaware of the difference when explaining distances in English.

Fuel. Petrol costs about SEK 14 per litre and diesel SEK 12. Many petrol stations have automatic 24-hour pumps, which take cards as well as 20, 50 and 100 SEK notes (although not for diesel).

Accidents and breakdowns. For emergency car repairs, call Assistancekåren, tel: 020-912 912;for nationwide motor assistance, tel: 08-627 5757; www.assistancekaren.se.

Serious accidents, especially if there are injuries, warrant use of the **112** emergency number for the police. Although it is not mandatory to call the police to an accident, even if damage is slight drivers must give their name and contact address to others involved before leaving the scene. Drivers who do not stop after an accident are liable to a fine or, in certain cases, imprisonment.

International pictographs are widely used on road signs, although you may see some signs in Swedish.

ticket machine **biljettautomat**
bus lane **bussfil**
bus stop **busshållplats**
no through traffic **ej genomfart**
private parking **privat parkering**
driving licence **körkort**

Other Useful Vocabulary:

car registration papers **besiktningsinstrument**
Please check the oil/tyres/battery. **Kan ni kontrollera oljan/ däcken/batteriet, tack.**
I've broken down. **Bilen har gått sönder.**
There's been an accident. **Det har hänt en olycka.**

E

ELECTRICITY

Swedish electricity is 220 volts AC and requires standard two-pin, round continental plugs. Visitors should bring their own adapters. Laptop computers that can function on both 110 and 220 volts can be used just with an adapter; those that work only on 110 volts will also need a transformer.

EMBASSIES AND CONSULATES *(ambassad; konsulat)*

UK: Skarpögatan 6-8, 115 93 Stockholm; tel: 08-671 30 00; http://
ukinsweden.fco.gov.uk.

USA: Dag Hammarskjöldsväg 31, 115 89 Stockholm; tel: 08-783 53
00; http://sweden.usembassy.gov.

Canada: Klarabergsgatan 23, 6th Floor, 103 23 Stockholm; tel: 08-
453 3000; www.sweden.gc.ca.

Australia: Klarabergsviadukten 63, 8th Floor, 101 36 Stockholm;
tel: 08-613 2900; www.sweden.embassy.gov.au.

South Africa: Fleminggatan 20, 4th Floor, 112 26 Stockholm; tel:
08- 243 950; www.southafrica.se.

Ireland: Hovslagargatan 5, 111 48 Stockholm; tel: 08-5450 4040;
www.embassyofireland.se.

Most embassies are open 9am–4.30pm (closed for lunch), but
there is usually someone on duty 24 hours a day. Telephone in advance if in doubt.

EMERGENCIES (See also POLICE)

For the police, fire brigade or ambulance, dial **112** from anywhere
in Sweden. Calls are free from payphones.

ETIQUETTE (See also TIPPING)

If you're travelling with children, note that smacking children is
illegal in Sweden.

G

GAY AND LESBIAN TRAVELLERS

Sweden is one of the world's most progressive countries when it
comes to gay rights. Information and advice can be obtained from
the Swedish Federation for Lesbian, Gay, Bisexual and Transgen-
der Rights: RFSL, Sveavägen 59; tel: 08-501 62 900; www.rfsl.se.
Also see the online gay entertainment guide, www.qx.se.

GETTING THERE

Air. Scandinavia's flag carrier, SAS (www.sas.se), most main European and several North American airlines fly into Stockholm's Arlanda Airport. SAS and a few smaller operators offer internal connections to all parts of the country. Gothenburg's Landvetter and Malmö's Sturup airports have some international flights and also connections to the internal network. Low-cost carriers include Ryanair (www.ryanair.com), Norwegian (www.norwegian.com) and WizzAir (https://wizzair.com).

Sea. From Britain, DFDS Seaways (www.dfdsseaways.com) sails Harwich–Esbjerg throughout the year. From Germany, the main routes are Rostock–Trelleborg, Kiel–Gothenburg, Travemünde–Malmö or Travemünde–Trelleborg. From Denmark: Frederikshavn–Gothenburg, Helsingør–Helsingborg and Grenaa–Varberg. The Oresund Bridge connects Copenhagen and Malmö, providing access for both cars and trains. There are also services between Stockholm and Helsinki, Russia and the Baltic States.

Rail. The main Continental cities are linked to Sweden by rail. To reach Stockholm from London (St Pancras), take the Eurostar to Brussels, then onwards via Hamburg or Cologne and Copenhagen. A slower option is from London (Liverpool Street) via Harwich and the Harwich–Esbjerg ferry, which connects with a train to Stockholm via Copenhagen.

Road. Many countries are connected to Sweden by coach. London to Stockholm, via Amsterdam, takes over 40 hours. From London it is also possible to travel with your car via the Channel Tunnel to France, from where you can continue your journey by road – a distance of some 1,800km (1,120 miles).

GUIDES AND TOURS

English is Sweden's second language, which makes it easy to get an English-speaking guide. German-speaking guides are almost as plentiful. Bus or boat tours are multilingual, as are those in some museums and other places of interest. Local tourist offices can also make bookings for tours and guides, or tell you where to book. In Stockholm authorised guides can be booked at www.visitstockholm.com or by ringing the Stockholm Tourist Service at 08-1200 4979; www.stotourist.se.

H

HEALTH AND MEDICAL CARE (See also EMERGENCIES)

No vaccinations are needed for Sweden. Tap water is safe to drink.

The country does not have the equivalent of the general-practice surgery. If you become ill, ask your hotel to call a doctor who is affiliated to *Försäkringskassan* (Swedish National Health Service). If you are able, go to the casualty department, *Akutmottagning*, at a hospital, or *Vårdcentral* (health centre) in more rural areas. Bring your passport or ID, health insurance and European Health Insurance Card (if applicable). Take a doctor's prescription for medicines to any chemist *(apotek)*. These are open during shopping hours.

Late-night chemists. Call 0771-450 450 for more information.

Stockholm: C.W. Scheele, Klarabergsgatan 64; open 24 hours, including holidays.

Gothenburg: Apoteket Smörblomman, Östra sjukhuset, Smörslottsgatan 1; open to 10pm daily.

Malmö: Apoteket Gripen, Bergsgatan 48; open to 11pm daily.

Dental treatment. *Tandläkare* means dental surgery.

Emergency services in larger cities are shown on the health, or 'blue', pages of the business phone directory. Sweden has a reciprocal agreement for medical treatment with other EU countries, giving entitlement to the same emergency service as Swedes.

L

LANGUAGE

Most Swedes speak excellent English, a little less so in remote areas. German is the next choice of language and is spoken by many (particularly in the tourist industry). Menus in city restaurants often give English translations.

Although Swedish is pleasant to hear, it is not easy to pronounce and the language has three extra vowels: å, ä and ö (listed as the last three letters of the alphabet).

Useful Expressions

big/small **stor/liten**	next/last **nästa/sista**
quick/slow **snabb/långsam**	good/bad **bra/dålig**
hot/cold **varm/kall**	early/late **tidig/sen**
heavy/light **tung/lätt**	cheap/expensive **billig/dyr**
open/shut **öpen/stängd**	near/far **nära/långt (bort)**
right/wrong **rätt/fel**	here/there **här/där**
old/new **gammal/ny**	

Days of the Week

Sunday **söndag**	Thursday **torsdag**
Monday **måndag**	Friday **fredag**
Tuesday **tisdag**	Saturday **lördag**
Wednesday **onsdag**	

Months

January **januari**	July **juli**
February **februari**	August **augusti**
March **mars**	September **september**
April **april**	October **oktober**
May **maj**	November **november**
June **juni**	December **december**

MEDIA

Newspapers and magazines (*tidning; tidskrift*). Sweden's main daily newspapers are *Svenska Dagbladet*, *Dagens Nyheter* and *Göteborgs Posten* (broadsheets), and *Expressen* and *Aftonbladet* (tabloids), all in Swedish. English-language newspapers are on sale in kiosks and central stations. Stockholm's Kulturhuset (Culture House) has a selection of English-language newspapers to read on the premises, as do the city libraries in Stockholm and Gothenburg. Some of the top hotels offer them on a complimentary basis. For Swedish news in English, visit www. thelocal.se.

Radio and television. *Sveriges Radio* (Radio Sweden) and *Sveriges Television* (Swedish Television) are the main companies. *Sveriges Radio* broadcasts regular 30-minute programmes of news and information in English, which can be heard online (www.sr.se) and at 3pm Monday to Friday on the P2 radio channel, and also at 8.30pm Monday to Friday in the Stockholm area on FM 89.6MHz. Most hotels carry English-language satellite channels such as CNN, plus German-language channels direct from Germany.

MONEY

Currency. Swedish currency is the *krona* (or 'crown'; plural *kronor*), made up of 100 *öre*. It is abbreviated kr or SEK (the international abbreviation). Coins come in 1, 5 and 10 kronor. Lighter copper-coloured 1-, 2- and gold-coloured 5-krona coins will be introduced in October 2016, which will also see the arrival of newly designed 100- and 500-krona banknotes. Current bank notes are 20-, 50-, 200- and 1,000-krona banknotes. Old 20-, 50- and 1000-krona banknotes will be discontinued after 30 June 2016. A year later, on 30 June 2017, the 100-krona and

500-krona banknotes and 1-, 2- and 5-krona coins will become invalid. Novel banknotes will be equipped with state-of-the-art security features and will depict Swedish prominent 20th-century figures, for example the 200-krona note will feature Ingmar Bergman. For more information visit the website of Sweden's central bank: www.riksbank.se.

Exchange facilities. You can change currency at airports; the central stations in Malmö, Stockholm and Gothenburg; almost all commercial and savings banks; post offices; branches of Forex (bureaux de change); hotels; and some department stores.

Credit cards. Most major credit cards are widely accepted, although some restaurants may not take American Express cards.

Traveller's cheques. Banks and hotels will change traveller's cheques or cash, but banks usually give a better rate. Shops generally accept traveller's cheques for purchases.

O

OPENING TIMES (See also PUBLIC HOLIDAYS)

Shops: Weekday opening 10am–6pm; Sat 10am–2pm or 4pm. Some big stores and shopping centres in larger towns stay open until 7pm or later, and may also open noon–4pm Sun. In rural areas, closing time for shops and petrol stations is usually 5 or 6pm. Shops close early the day before a public holiday.

Banks: 10am–3pm Mon–Fri; in larger cities some stay open until 5.30pm. Banks at the main airports open later.

P

POLICE (*polis*; see also EMERGENCIES)

Main police stations are open weekdays and have a public desk for incidents, thefts or other problems, and usually a lost-property office. Stockholm police station is at Bergsgatan 48: for other police-station addresses and opening hours, see www. polisen.se. For non-emergencies, tel: 114 14.

The emergency police number (also fire, ambulance, etc.) is 112; free when calling from a payphone.

POST OFFICES *(postkontor)*

Post offices are now integrated with selected grocery stores, kiosks and petrol stations; look for the blue postal sign. Opening hours vary depending on the specific store. There are two different types of mailboxes: the blue box is for local deliveries and the yellow for national and international deliveries. In Stockholm, the post office at Centralstationen opens Mon–Fri 5.30am–11pm, Sat–Sun 8am–11pm; www.posten.se.

PUBLIC HOLIDAYS *(helgdagar;* see also OPENING TIMES)

Banks, shops and offices close on the public holidays listed below, and may also close earlier the day before (eg. Twelfth Night (5 January), Midsummer Eve, Christmas Eve, New Year's Eve). Cinemas, museums and restaurants may stay open on public holidays. The country grinds to a standstill on 24 December, the day Swedes celebrate Christmas.

New Year's Day *Nyårsdagen* **1 January**
Epiphany *Trettondagen* **6 January**
May Day *Första Maj* **1 May**
Sweden's National Day *Sveriges nationaldagen* **6 June**
Midsummer Day *Midsommarsdagen* **Sat between 21 and 26 June**
All Saints' Day *Alla helgons dagen* **Sat between 31 Oct and 6 Nov**
Christmas Day *Juldagen* **25 December**
Boxing Day *Annandag jul* **26 December**
Movable Dates:
Good Friday *Långfredagen* **late March/early April**

Easter Sunday/Easter Monday *Påskdagen/Annandagpåsk* **late March/ early April**
Ascension Day *Kristi himmelsfårdsdagen* **May**
Whit Sunday *Pingstdagen* **May**

T

TELEPHONES *(telefon)*

To call Sweden from abroad, dial your country's international access code (00 from the UK; 011 from the US or Canada), followed by the Sweden country code 46, followed by the Swedish telephone number including the area code (but dropping the initial '0' of the area code, which is only used when dialling within Sweden).

To call abroad from within Sweden, dial the international access code 00, followed by the correct country code and telephone number (dropping the initial '0' of the area code for UK numbers).

To call local numbers from within Sweden, dial the telephone number including the full area code.

The rise in mobile-phone usage has seen a sharp decline in the number of public telephones – you may still find them however at railway stations, airports and petrol stations. Phone-cards can be purchased at newsagents (eg Pressbyrån) as well as at supermarkets. Some phones accept credit cards, indicated by 'CCC'.

Swedish mobile phones operate on the 900/1800 Mhz GSM network – most modern smartphones are compatible. The cheapest way to use your own mobile phone (although it must be unlocked) is to buy a Swedish SIM card from a newsagent – ask for a *startpaket*. Local mobile network operators include Tele2 (www.tele2.se), Telenor (www.telenor.se), Telia (www.telia.se) and 3 (www.tre.se).

TIME ZONES

Sweden keeps Central European Time, one hour ahead of Greenwich Mean Time. Clocks go forward by one hour during the summer (late March to late October).

New York	London	Paris	**Stockholm**	Sydney	Auckland
6am	11am	noon	**noon**	8pm	10pm

TIPPING

Egalitarian Sweden is not a tipping nation. However, restaurant bills are usually rounded up to the nearest SEK 10 or SEK 20, and it's becoming more common to leave a further tip for good service.

It is customary to round up the taxi fare to the nearest SEK 10. Add 10 percent if, for example, the driver carries a case up a flight of stairs. When you leave a coat in a cloakroom, the charge is usually SEK 15–20 per article.

TOURIST INFORMATION OFFICES

Sweden has an excellent network of tourist offices *(turistbyråer)* in 300 towns and cities, identified by the international tourist 'i' sign. About half sport a blue-and-yellow (rather than a green) 'i' sign: these provide a more comprehensive service.

Stockholm Visitors Board, Visitor Center, Sergels Torg 5, Stockholm; tel: 08-508 285 08; www.visitstockholm.com.

Gothenburg Tourist Office, Kungsportsplatsen 2, Göteborg; tel: 031-368 42 00; www.goteborg.com.

Malmö Tourism, Börshuset, Skeppsbron 2, Malmö ; tel: 040-34 12 00; www.visitmalmo.com, www.malmotown.com.

Visit Sweden, tel: 08-789 10 00; www.visitsweden.com.

Overseas Offices

Great Britain: Visit Sweden; tel: 020-7108 6168.

USA: Visit Sweden, PO Box 4649, Grand Central Station, New York NY 10163-4649; tel: 212-885 9700.

TRANSPORT

Sweden has good and well-maintained bus and rail services. Long distances make domestic airlines almost a necessity.

Buses *(bussar)*. Swebus (tel: 0771-218 218; www.swebus.se) is the largest intercity operator, operating express bus services between larger towns in Southern and Central Sweden and between Stockholm and the northern coastal towns. Buy tickets before travelling, by phone, from rail and bus stations, and from 7-Eleven and Pressbyrån shops. Svenska Buss (tel: 0771-67 67 67; www.svenskabuss.se) also runs some services in the south.

In cities, the bus services are frequent, comprehensive and well integrated with other transport. Stockholm's bus network is the largest in the world, run by SL (Storstockholms Lokaltrafik; tel: 08-600 10 00; www.sl.se), which also operates integrated underground and local train services. Gothenburg has an ecologically friendly tram network.

Trains *(tåg)*. The Swedish state railway SJ (tel: 0771-75 75 75; www.sj.se) covers the whole country, using several different types of train. High-speed *(snabbtåg)* trains, for example on the Stockholm–Gothenburg route, require advance reservations; InterCity trains also provide a fast service; Regional and Lokaltog trains are the slowest and cheapest. Long-distance trains have restaurant cars and/or buffets, and there are also sleepers and couchettes for both first and second class. Tickets can be booked online at the SJ website.

Inlandsbanan (Inland Railway; tel: 0771-53 53 53; www.inlands banan.com), a special scenic line, runs from Kristinehamn in the south to Gällivare beyond the Arctic Circle with stops and excursions (see page 78).

Taxis *(taxi)*. Taxi ranks are marked *taxi*, but you can also hail taxis on the street. A lit sign, *ledig*, means a taxi is free. You can also book by phone or online, e.g. on www.taxi020.se in Stockholm, Gothenburg and Malmö. Taxis have meters and willingly issue receipts. Credit cards are accepted.

Underground *(Tunnelbana)*. SL (http://sl.se) runs the Stockholm underground, *Tunnelbana* or *T-banan*, which covers 110km (68 miles) of track and incorporates 100 stations. These are marked with a large 'T' and are very clean. Stockholm also runs a good system of local trains.

Ferries and boats *(färja; båt)*. Many islands have regular connections, one of the busiest ports being the Baltic island of Gotland. There are also scheduled boats in and around the Stockholm archipelago and in other coastal areas, in addition to regular services. Big lakes, such as Vänern, Vättern, Mälaren, Siljan, Storsjön and others, also have services.

Resplus (www.samtrafiken.se) combines information from all the Swedish transport companies about rail, bus and boat journeys, and is therefore a good website to visit if your journey is complicated.

V

VISAS AND ENTRY REQUIREMENTS

EU and North American visitors need only a valid passport (or ID, if they reside in a Schengen Area country) to stay in Sweden for up to three months. Other nationalities should check with their nearest Swedish embassy. Regulations can change, so always check before you travel.

Duty-free. For residents of EU-member countries, precise restrictions have been lifted on the quantities of alcohol and tobacco that can be imported, but the goods have to be for personal use. Customs officers decide whether the quantities cross the line into commercial-import quantities.

W

WEBSITES AND INTERNET ACCESS

www.visitsweden.com Official VisitSweden tourist information, with links to regional tourist-office websites

www.sweden.se Information on culture, tourism, business, society.

www.thelocal.se Swedish news in English.

www.visitstockholm.com Official Stockholm tourist information.

www.goteborg.com Official Gothenburg tourist information.

www.stayinsweden.com Hotel booking site.

www.swedishepa.se/en National parks and countryside access.

www.kungahuset.se Royal palaces and gardens.

Y

YOUTH HOSTELS *(vandrarhem)*

Sweden has over 400 hostels in buildings from manor houses to former prisons (Långholmen in Stockholm), catering for everyone from single travellers to families. Some are open only in summer.

Most hostels are run by Svenska Turistföreningen (Swedish Tourist Club – STF; www.svenskaturistforeningen.se), who also offer camping packages, as well as operating mountain cabins where you bring your own food, and small boat harbours, and advising about cycling hire and holidays. Members of other countries' hostel associations qualify for cheap rates if they produce their membership cards. The normal price is SEK 130–230 per night, plus SEK 50 for non-members. You should provide sheets or sheet sleeping bags but can also buy or hire them.

Around 185 independent hostels belong to the association SVIF (www.svif.se). Their brochure can also be downloaded or picked up from any tourist office in Sweden.

In summer, it's smart to book ahead, as this form of holiday is very popular.

RECOMMENDED HOTELS

Sweden has many hotels in many places, so it is impossible to cover every area in full. This list gives a selection in the three main cities, plus a few in more widespread areas. In the north in particular, except in towns, hotels may be far apart. In central and north Sweden many hotels and inns also have self-catering *stugor* for two to six people in their grounds. Hostel-style accommodation is not uncommon in the wilderness areas.

Hotels are of a high standard, but not cheap. Most are completely smoke-free.

The price categories below are based on two people sharing a double room at full rates, including breakfast, MOMS (tax) and service charge.

$$$	above SEK 2,200
$$	SEK 1,200–2,200
$	below SEK 1,200

STOCKHOLM

Berns Hotel $$$ *Näckströmsgatan 8, 111-47 Stockholm; tel: 08-566 322 00*; www.berns.se. Centrally located, historic boutique hotel, with on-site restaurants and a nightclub. Many of its modern rooms have balconies. The hotel also boasts a magnificent breakfast hall with crystal chandeliers.

Castanea Old Town Hostel $ *Kindstugatan 1, Gamla Stan, 111-31 Stockholm; tel: 08-22 35 51*; www.castaneavandrarhem.se. Small, very well-kept hostel in the heart of the cobbled Old Town.

Elite Hotel Stockholm Plaza $$–$$$ *Birger Jarlsgatan 29, 111-45 Stockholm; tel: 08-566 220 00*; www.elite.se. Unusual, stone-built 19th-century hotel with a pleasant atmosphere. Surrounded by shops and outdoor cafés; handy for the centre and close to Humlegård Park.

First Hotel Reisen $$–$$$ *Skeppsbron 12–14, 111-30 Stockholm; tel: 08-22 32 60*; www.firsthotels.com. Well-known 19th-century hotel on the waterfront in Gamla Stan, with fine view towards Saltsjön and an acclaimed cocktail bar.

Grand Hôtel $$$ *Södra Blasieholmshamnen 8, 103-27 Stockholm; tel: 08-679 35 00;* www.grandhotel.se. Luxury hotel overlooking the water to Gamla Stan and the Royal Palace. Michelin-starred restaurant.

Hilton Stockholm Slussen $$–$$$ *Guldgränd 8, 104-65 Stockholm; tel: 08-517 353 00;* www.hilton.co.uk/stockholm. Bright, pleasant accommodation. Book a room with views over the water to the Old Town; otherwise, enjoy the panoramic bars and restaurants.

Hotell Diplomat $$–$$$ *Strandvägen 7C, 104-40 Stockholm; tel: 08-459 68 00;* www.diplomathotel.com. Built in Jugend style with crisp decor and soothing rooms, this classy waterfront hotel has plenty of character. Sit on your balcony and watch the boats go by.

Hotell Mälardrottningen $–$$ *Riddarholmen, 111-28 Stockholm; tel: 08-545 187 80;* www.malardrottningen.se. This unusual boat hotel is based in a 1920s luxury yacht formerly owned by American millionairess Barbara Hutton. Situated in lovely anchorage at Riddarholmen, there's a gourmet restaurant and 61 cabins, from 6 to 17 sq metres!

Långholmen $–$$ *Långholmsmuren 20, 117-33 Stockholm; tel: 08-720 85 00;* www.langholmen.com. Unusual hotel and youth hostel, in a former prison and set apart on its own wooded island. The nearest metro station is Hornstull, five stops from the central railway station.

Mornington Hotel $$ *Nybrogatan 53, 102-44 Stockholm; tel: 08-507 330 00;* www.mornington.se. Central hotel, close to museums, with a charming design, friendly atmosphere, and books everywhere. Superb weekend brunches.

Scandic Hasselbacken Hotel $$–$$$ *Hazeliusbacken 20, 100-55 Stockholm; tel: 08-517 343 00;* www.scandichotels.se. Scandic have nine hotels in the centre of Stockholm – see the website for details. This one is on the green island Djurgården, handy for Skansen, Gröna Lund and the Vasa museum. It's popular with families.

Story Hotel $$–$$$ *Riddargatan 6, 114-35 Stockholm; tel: 08-545 039 40;* www.storyhotels.com. Opened in 2009, this design-savvy boutique hotel has a central location, great service and a truly off-beat feel.

Victory Hotel $$$ *Lilla Nygatan 5, 111-28 Stockholm; tel: 08-506 400 50;* www.thecollectorshotels.se. In a 17th-century building on a quiet street, close to Mälaren. Nautical antiques and an 18th-century design sensibility lend the hotel a country-house atmosphere.

AROUND STOCKHOLM

Grand Hotel Saltsjöbaden $$ *133-83 Saltsjöbaden; tel: 08-506 170 00;* www.grandsaltsjobaden.se. It may have seen better days, but this ornate castle-like hotel has a fantastic location in the heart of the Stockholm archipelago.

Gripsholms Värdshus and Hotel $$$ *Kyrkogatan 1, 647-30 Mariefred; tel: 0159-347 50;* www.gripsholms-vardshus.se. This historic inn, on the shores of Lake Mälaren, first threw open its doors in the 17th century. Some of its comfortable rooms have wonderful views of Gripsholm Slott, across the water.

Radisson Blu Uppsala $$ *Stationsgatan 4, 753-40 Uppsala; tel: 018-47 47 900;* www.radissonblu.com/hotel-uppsala. Brand-new in 2012, this up-market business hotel is right opposite the train station. Clean, bright rooms have air-conditioning as standard.

Sigtuna Stadshotell $$$ *Stora Nygatan 3, 193-30 Sigtuna; tel: 08-592 501 00;* www.sigtunastadshotell.se. A small, elegant hotel in central Sigtuna. Many of its rooms, decorated in calming Gustavian style with modern details, have lake views.

Vandrarhem Uppsala Kungsängstorg & Hotell Kungsängstorg $ *Kungsängstorg 6, 753-20 Uppsala; tel: 018-444 20 10;* www.vandrarhem uppsala.se. For a less corporate stay, this central family-run hotel and youth hostel is a winner. The classically proportioned 19th-century building boasts wooden floors and gnarled roof-beams, giving its rooms a cosy, rustic feel.

Waxholms Hotell $$ *Hamngatan 2, 185-21 Vaxholm; tel: 08-541 301 50;* www.waxholmshotell.se. A warm and friendly family-run spot on Vaxholm island. Enjoy hypnotic harbour views from the restaurant.

MALMÖ AND THE SOUTH

Hotel Concordia $-$$ *Stålbrogatan 1, 222-24 Lund; tel: 046-13 50 50;* www.concordia.se. In heart of Lund's medieval town, Concordia is a pleasant family-run option.

Hotel Mäster Johan $$ *Mäster Johansgatan 13, 211-21 Malmö; tel: 040-664 6400;* www.masterjohan.se. First-class hotel with a friendly atmosphere in central Malmö.

More Hotel $ *Norra Skolgatan 24, 214-22 Malmö; tel: 040-665 1000;* www.themorehotel.se. A home-away-from-home, this good-value option offers comfortable studio apartments (with kitchenette, living room and bedroom) for stays from one night to six months.

Radisson Blu Hotel, Malmö $$ *Östergatan 10, 211-25 Malmö; tel: 040-698 4000;* www.radissonblu.com/en/hotel-malmo. Fresh, spacious rooms, popular with business travellers. A short walk to Malmö centre, or dine on the premises at the recommended restaurant.

Slottshotellet $-$$ *Slottsvägen 7, 392-33 Kalmar; tel: 0480-882 60;* www.slottshotellet.se. Views over Kalmarsund and next to castle park. Good-value budget rooms in summer in an annexe.

BALTIC ISLANDS

Best Western Strand Hotel Visby $$ *Strandgatan 34, 621-56 Visby, Gotland; tel: 0498-25 88 00;* www.strandhotel.se. An average hotel with a great location – within Visby's medieval walls and close to the shore and the botanic gardens. Small indoor pool.

Halltorps Gästgiveri $$ *Landsvägen Halltorp 105, 387-92 Borgholm, Öland; tel: 0485-850 00;* www.halltorpsgastgiveri.se. In a 17th-century inn, 9km (6 miles) from Borgholm on Öland, overlooking Kalmar Sound. The 'mansion' rooms are a cut above the rest, with stylish furniture and original artworks.

GOTHENBURG

Hotel Royal $$ *Drottninggatan 67, 411-07 Göteborg; tel: 031-700 11 70; www.hotel-royal.com.* Gothenburg's oldest hotel is an Art-Nouveau gem, located conveniently close to the railway station. It tries hard to please, with charming staff, and free coffee and cake supplied to guests in the afternoon.

Hotell Liseberg Heden $$ *Sten Sturegatan, 411-39 Göteborg; tel: 031-750 69 00; www.liseberg.se.* Located in the Heden (heath) district, a green area within easy walking distance of the Avenyn. Discount tickets to Liseberg theme park are available for hotel guests. Popular with families.

Hotell Riverton $$ *Stora Badhusgatan 26, 411-21 Göteborg; tel: 031-750 10 00; www.hotellriverton.se.* Close to the north harbour and Opera House. There's a view of the estuary from the 11th-storey Sky Bar. Rooms are smart and fresh.

Spar Hotel Majorna $ *Karl Johansgatan 66–70, 414-54 Göteborg; tel: 031-751 07 00; www.sparhotel.se.* Cosy hotel near old Majorna harbour. Sauna, trams to the centre, free parking. Good rooms at budget price.

THE WEST

Clarion Collection Hotel Kung Oscar $–$$ *Drottninggatan 17, 461-32 Trollhättan; tel: 0520-70 470; www.nordicchoicehotels.com.* Centrally located in Trollhättan, the hotel offers opulently decorated, modern rooms. A complimentary light evening meal served between 6pm and 9pm is included in the price.

Ronnums Herrgård $$ *Parkvägen 18, 468-30 Vargön, near Vänersborg; tel: 0521-26 00 00; www.ronnumsherrgard.se.* Superb manor house in parkland south of Lake Vänern. Celebrated for its gourmet food, informality and good service. Golf packages, and occasional chocolate-/wine-tasting weekends.

Tanums Gestgifveri $$ *Apoteksvägen 7, 457-32 Tanumshede; tel: 0525-290 10;* www.hoteltanum.se. Charming 17th-century inn, close to famous prehistoric carvings and beautiful fishing villages. Golf packages are available.

Vadstena Klosterhotel $$ *Lasarettsgatan 5, 592-24 Vadstena; tel: 0143-315 30;* www.klosterhotel.se. One of Sweden's oldest hotels, next door to St Birgitta Kyrka on Lake Vättern, decorated in simple whitewashed style as befits its medieval-convent heritage. The same team runs several more opulent properties (Renaissance, Gustavian and Art Nouveau) around Vadstena.

THE CENTRAL HEARTLANDS

Åkerblads Hotell och Gästgiveri $$ *Sjögattu 2, 793-70 Tällberg; tel: 0247-508 00;* www.akerblads.se. The Åkerblad family have owned this building since the 1700s. Great restaurant, pool and spa treatments.

Best Western Hotel Söderhamn $$ *Montörsbacken 4, 826-40 Söderhamn; tel: 0270-26 62 00;* www.hotellsoderh.se. Well-furnished hotel with modern facilities, just off the E4. Restaurant with taverna-style fare.

Clarion Hotel Grand $$ *Prästgatan 16, 831-31 Östersund; tel: 063-55 60 00;* www.nordicchoicehotels.no. Good hotel in a central position on Stortorget, with a restaurant and swimming pool.

Elite Hotel Knaust $$ *Storgatan 13, 852-30 Sundsvall; tel: 060-608 00 00;* www.elite.se. An impressive historical interior has been gracefully melded with modern comfort and stylish contemporary touches. Popular restaurant and bar.

Fryksås Hotell & Gestgifveri $$ *794-90 Orsa; tel: 0250-460 20;* www.fryksashotell.se. On high southern slopes above lakes Siljan and Orsasjön, the hotel rooms and mountain chalets here have fine views. Its gourmet restaurant uses local wild ingredients. Around 6km (4 miles) from Grönklitt Bear Park and ski area.

Hotel Diplomat Åregården $$ *Åre Torg, 830-14 Åre; tel: 0647-178 00;* www.aregarden.se. A charming turn-of-the-century hotel and ski lodge right in the centre of Åre. Sauna and good après-ski, as well as restaurants and nightclubs.

Tänndalen Fjällhotell $–$$ *Rörosvägen 466, 840-98 Tänndalen; tel: 0684-220 20;* www.hotelltanndalen.se. Family-run establishment in a popular all-year mountain resort area. Excellent food, wonderful mountain panorama and indoor pool; outdoor activities available. Miles of ski tracks close by.

Järvsöbaden Hotell $$ *820-40 Järvsö; tel: 0651-404 00;* www.jarvs obaden.se. Rural hotel owned and run by the same family since it was built in 1905. On Öjeberget mountain, close to Järvsö Zoo on the outskirts of town. The grounds are lovely and contain a swimming pool.

Södra Berget $$ *Södra Stadsberget, 851-24 Sundsvall; tel: 060-67 10 00;* www.sodraberget.se. Wonderful position at the top of Södra Berget, one of Sundsvall's two outlook hills, 3km (2 miles) from the centre. Fabulous views, sauna, fitness room, slalom run, walking and skiing.

NORRLAND AND THE ARCTIC

Amber Hotell $ *Stationsgatan 67, 972-34 Luleå; tel: 0920-102 00;* www. amber-hotell.se. Small and sweet, this good-value family hotel has just 16 rooms, and is handy for the railway station and town centre. Bike and skate rental.

Hotel Arctic Eden $–$$ *Föraregatan 18, 981-39 Kiruna; tel: 0980-611 86;* www.hotelarcticeden.se. Charming hotel in the old schoolhouse, with close connections to Sami culture. Bright, clean rooms, plenty of activities and just a five-minute walk from central Kiruna. Tiny indoor swimming pool.

Hotel Jokkmokk $–$$ *Solgatan 45, 962-31 Jokkmokk; tel: 0971-777 00;* www.hoteljokkmokk.se. A good hotel in the heart of Sami country, with a lake-view restaurant that serves local specialities. Can help arrange activities including elk safaris, snowmobile excursions and fishing instruction.

Hotel Pilen $ *Pilgatan 5, 903-31 Umeå; tel: 090-14 46 60;* www.hotell pilen.se. Small and cosy 22-room budget hotel, decorated with much more colour and personality than the average Swedish hotel. A short walk from the town centre.

Hotell Laponia $$ *Storgatan 45, 933-33 Arvidsjaur; tel: 0960-555 00;* www.hotell-laponia.se. A large and fairly comfortable modern hotel, close to Arvidsjaur's main lake, this makes a good base for rafting, walking, dogsledding and skiing. The restaurant serves Norrland specialities.

Hotell Nordkalotten $–$$ *Lulviksvägen 1, 972-54 Luleå; tel: 0920-20 00 00;* www.nordkalotten.com. Dark wood and taxidermied birds and beasts lend a gothic air to this cabin-in-the-woods, on the edge of town beside a small lake. More expensive rooms have private mini-saunas. Perfect for walkers and cross-country skiers. Indoor pool.

Hotell Silverhatten $$ *930-90 Arjeplog; tel: 0961-107 70;* www.silver hatten.se. Sitting on a mountain above town, most of Silverhatten's recently renovated rooms (and panoramic restaurant) have endless views. Open November to April. The resort also offers accommodation in the high-quality hotel rooms and holiday cabins of the water-side Kraja resort, 1.5km away.

Ice Hotel $$–$$$ *981-91 Jukkasjärvi; tel: 0980-66 800;* www.icehotel. se. Choose to sleep on reindeer skins in an ice-room – definitely a unique experience – or in a standard, warm hotel room. The hotel is carved from ice every year by artists from across the globe. Top-quality restaurant.

Lövånger Kyrkstad $ *Kungsvägen 31, 930-10 Lövånger; tel: 0913-102 03;* www.lovangerkyrkstad.se. For something a little different, try this restored church village where guests sleep in tiny, beautifully refurbished 17th-century cottages. Restaurant on site.

INDEX

Berlitz POCKET GUIDE

SWEDEN

Twelfth Edition 2016

Editor: Kate Drynan
Author: Doreen Taylor-Wilkie
Head of Production: Rebeka Davies
Picture Editor: Tom Smyth
Cartography Update: Carte
Update Production: AM Services
Photography Credits: Andreas Nordström/imagebank.sweden.se 5TC; Conny Fridh/imagebank.sweden.se 92, 95; Ewa-Maria Rundquist/The Royal Court of Sweden 24; Fredrik Broman/imagebank.sweden.se 102; Fredrik Nyman/imagebank.sweden.se 98; Göran Assner/imagebank.sweden.se 4BR, 54, 58; Henrik trygg/imagebank.sweden.se 86; Human Spectra/imagebank.sweden.se 82; iStock 4TL, 73; Jan Lindblad Jr/Apa Publications 18; Jessica Lindgren/imagebank.sweden.se 4TC, 77; Julian Love/Apa Publications 4ML, 5T, 5MC, 6TL, 6TL, 6MC, 6ML, 7T, 7T, 7M, 7MC, 8L, 8R, 9, 11, 15, 16, 21, 22, 26, 29, 30, 32, 34, 36, 39, 40, 45, 47, 63, 65, 66, 69, 70, 84, 89, 96, 101, 104; Justin Brown/imagebank.sweden.se 4/5M, 42/43; Magnus Skoglöf/imagebank.sweden.se 102/103; Melker Dahlstrand/imagebank.sweden.se 49; Nicho Södling/imagebank.sweden.se 60, 90; Ola Ericson/imagebank.sweden.se 12; Patrick Tragardh/imagebank.sweden.se 5MC; Paul Panayiotou/Corbis 93; Peter Grant/imagebank.sweden.se 79; Rodrigo Rivas Ruiz/imagebank.sweden.se 94; Staffan Widstrand/imagebank.sweden.se 74; Tuukka Ervasti/imagebank.sweden.se 9R, 51, 53; Tomas Utsi - www.naturfoto.se 5M, 81
Cover Picture: 4Corners

Distribution
UK: Dorling Kindersley Ltd,
A Penguin Group company, 80 Strand, London,
WC2R 0RL; sales@uk.dk.com
United States: Ingram Publisher Services,
1 Ingram Boulevard, PO Box 3006, La Vergne,
TN 37086-1986; ips@ingramcontent.com
Australia and New Zealand: Woodslane,
10 Apollo St, Warriewood, NSW 2102,
Australia; info@woodslane.com.au
Worldwide: Apa Publications (Singapore) Pte,
7030 Ang Mo Kio Avenue 5,
08-65 Northstar @ AMK, Singapore 569880
apasin@singnet.com.sg

Contact us
Every effort has been made to provide accurate information in this publication, but changes are inevitable. The publisher cannot be responsible for any resulting loss, inconvenience or injury. We would appreciate it if readers would call our attention to any errors or outdated information. We also welcome your suggestions; please contact us at: berlitz@apaguide.co.uk
www.insightguides.com/berlitz